Ruth Meredith Stella Stour

The Story of
COVENT GARDEN

Contents

List of Illustrations

Between pages 144 and 145

Acknoledgements

Grateful acknowledgement is made to the following for their kind permission to reproduce illustrations: Ashmolean Museum (31); Blackie & Son (3, 17); British Library (7, 13, 24); British Museum (4, 23, 25, 32); Covent Garden Market Authority (14, 15, 18, 45, 47); Guildhall Library (37); Museum of London (16, 20, 26, 27, 28, 29, 36, 38, 41, 42); National Portrait Gallery (2, 5, 6, 8, 9, 10, 11,

1

The Convent Garden

In the early Middle Ages the way from the walled city of London to St Peter's Abbey and the royal palace of Westminster lay along a lonely track, already known as the Strand, which ran between the muddy shores of the Thames and the fields and forests of Middlesex.

By the thirteenth century London had already spread beyond the confines of its Roman wall, and its boundaries enclosed nearly a square mile. The heart of the city was the Gothic cathedral of St Paul, and nearly a quarter of the square mile was taken up by the 120 little parish churches, with their graveyards and chantries. The prosperous shopkeepers and merchants lived in their timber-framed houses, two or three storeys high, the craftsmen in simple, two-roomed tenements, but the labourers, of whom there were some forty thousand by Chaucer's time, lived where they could, hopelessly overcrowded, in little shacks of timber and straw, run up haphazardly in the winding lanes and courtyards, with their open drains and piles of refuse, which grew up behind the larger dwellings.

Many noblemen also had their town houses in the city, most of them close to the river, built in the narrow lanes which ran steeply down to the water's edge; but as the population increased, the wealthy began to move westwards, along the Strand, building homes for themselves similar to those they had left, mainly of wood, with earth or brick walls protecting them from the roadway, and gardens behind running down to the water steps and the river. Here, on the south side of the Strand, rose the town houses of many of the earls and bishops, Essex House, Arundel House, Somerset House, the Palace of the Savoy, enlarged from the original home of Simon de Montfort, Durham House, York House and Suffolk House.

On the north side of the Strand there was little building, and it was still open country, apart from the small rectory house of the parish of St Clement Dane, which stood about where Catherine

Street now runs. Beyond it was a stretch of land which, since the thirteenth century, had belonged to the abbots of Westminster. This seven acres of 'fair spreading pasture', including the large field known as the Long Acre, they used partly as a burial ground for their convent – a term then used as much for a community of monks as of nuns – and partly as a kitchen garden for their daily needs of fruit and vegetables. At the western end was a small chapel for their use, which had been standing since Norman times, and beyond it, where Trafalgar Square now lies, were the royal mews, where the king's falconer kept the royal falcons.

As London spread westwards, the monks of Westminster began to sell the surplus product of their convent garden to the neighbouring households, and by about the fifteenth century they had enclosed it with a brick wall.

The western world was changing, slowly emerging from the long, dark, medieval years. In Rome and Florence began the Renaissance, a great revival of art and literature and a renewed interest in architecture and science, which was to influence the whole of Europe. In England, for the next two centuries, it manifested itself in a succession of brilliant artists, poets and playwrights.

With Henry VIII came the Reformation and the dissolution of the monasteries. Church lands were appropriated by the Crown and either sold or bestowed on favoured nobles. The convent garden in the Strand was given to Protector Somerset, but after his fall from grace and execution, it reverted to the Crown, and in 1552 Edward VI granted it to John Russell, the first Earl of Bedford.

For the next seventy years or more the Russells did nothing to develop their seven acres, but they built their town residence, Bedford House, about where Southampton Street now runs. It was still mainly a wooden building. Descriptions of it vary. One writer said it was 'but a mean wooden building, shut up from the street by an ordinary brick wall', but Strype described it as a 'large but old-built house, with a great yard before it for the reception of carriages, with a spacious garden having a terrace walk adjoining to the brick wall next the garden, behind which were coach-houses and stables'.

Henry VIII had already ordered the demolition of the monks' chapel, which had stood among the fields beyond the western boundary of the Russells' land, and in its place had ordered the building, at his own expense, of a new church, St

Martin-in-the-Fields, mainly because he disliked seeing the funerals of his subjects passing down Whitehall to their burial at Westminster. At the same time there was now a good deal of building on the north side of the Strand, to the east of the Bedford estate. Drury House was built where Drury Lane now runs, by Sir William Drury, a distinguished soldier who fought for Queen Elizabeth in the Irish wars but was to meet his death in a duel. It was a large house, approached by a pair of gates 'which leadeth into a large yard for the reception of coaches, and at the back of the house a handsome garden'.

A little to the west was Wimbledon House, the home of Viscount Wimbledon, a son of the Earl of Exeter, but it was burnt to the ground in 1628 and little more is known of it.

The little rectory house of St Clement Dane had come into the hands of Sir Thomas Palmer, who pulled it down and rebuilt it of 'brick and timber, very large and spacious'; but Palmer, having been a follower of the Duke of Somerset, was, in his turn, accused of high treason, and in 1553 met his end on Tower Hill. His house in the Strand was forfeited to the Crown, and Queen Elizabeth granted it to her Lord Treasurer, Sir William Cecil, later to become Lord Burleigh, who leased some land from the adjacent Bedford estate and enlarged it, calling it Burleigh House, a 'noble pile, built with brick, and adorned with four square turrets'. It faced the Strand, and its gardens ran from the west side of the garden wall of Wimbledon House to the green lane westwards which is now Southampton Street. Lord Burleigh died here in 1598, and the house passed to his son Thomas, created Earl of Exeter, so the house was henceforth known as Exeter House.

Yet the greater part of the Bedford estate – the convent garden – remained as it ever was. The Russell gardeners tended the orchard and vegetable garden and marketed their surplus produce, as the monks had done before them; and over the years people from neighbouring villages formed the habit of bringing their own wares to sell here, thereby creating for themselves an as yet unauthorized but very convenient market-place, which became established under the garden wall of Bedford House. The rest of the seven acres was let out to neighbouring members of the aristocracy for the stabling and pasturage of their horses, and a few small cottages were built there for the coachmen and ostlers, as well as the gardeners.

By 1560 the convent garden was a rectangular walled space, with a few trees and some three or four thatched cottages, bounded by open meadows to the north, by the enclosed Bedford House to the south, with Drury House, 'embosomed in green foliage', to the east, and on the west a leafy avenue known as St Martin's Lane, 'carrying the eye onwards into the country, towards the beautiful hills of Hampstead and Highgate', while the Strand itself, despite the mansions along its southern side, was 'full of pits and sloughs, very perilous and noisome', and between the Temple and the village of Charing it was 'so deep in mire as to be almost impassable, very noyous and foul, and in many places thereof very jeopardous to all people passing and repassing, as well on horseback as on foot, both in winter and in summer, by night and by day'.

The fashion for the play had grown quickly. The Universities and the Inns of Court all put on their plays, and a few professional companies appeared for the first time, each sponsored by a rich nobleman; in the early days they gave their performances in the courtyards of the inns, with the spectators mainly ranged in the surrounding galleries.

However, there was a growing Puritan movement in England, which was particularly strong in the City of London. The City Fathers disapproved of any form of play-acting, regarding it as the enactment of falsehoods. They exercised a strict censorship on the choice of the play and the place of its acting. They complained of dangerous crowding in the inns and the risk of spreading infection and plague, and also bewailed the fact that people were being tempted to take time off from work.

Boys took the women's parts, for the Puritan prejudice against women taking part in such mummeries was too strong to be resisted, although at the same time many thought it equally distasteful for boys to act as women. In any case, the players had a hard time to make ends meet, for despite their noble patrons, the inns took the money from the gallery audiences, and the players had to collect what they could from the people who crowded into the courtyard below to hear them.

At last, in 1575, the Lord Mayor and the aldermen forbade all players from performing within the limits of the City. The following year James Burbage borrowed enough money to build the first London theatre, choosing a site in Shoreditch, safely outside the City boundary and calling it simply 'The Theatre'. A few months later Philip Henslowe built 'The Curtain' close by. During the next few years several more theatres were built, and in 1599 Burbage built 'The Globe' on Bankside, for Shakespeare's plays. The nearby Paris Gardens was mainly a bear-garden but was also used, on occasion, for plays. In the country road behind Sir William Drury's house, already called Drury Lane, was one of London's cockpits, which also began to present plays from time to time. It was a rowdy sort of place, and on Shrove Tuesday of 1617 it was attacked by a crowd of London apprentices and very nearly demolished. This produced a broadsheet entitled: *A Ballade in praise of the London 'Prentices, and what they did at the Cockpit Playhouse in Drury Lane.*

Christopher Marlowe, who had been born in 1564, the same year as Shakespeare, arrived in London from Cambridge, found lodgings for himself in Shoreditch and presented his play *Tamburlaine The Great* to Philip Henslowe at 'The Curtain'. It was a flamboyant, ranting, violent drama, reeking with blood, and more compelling and vital than anything the English stage had yet seen; Henslowe accepted it at once. It was a brilliant success, and overnight Kit won fame.

Amongst those who came to meet him was Sir Walter Ralegh, who invited Kit to his London home, Durham House, in the Strand. Here, in his book-lined study, overlooking Bedford House and the fields of the convent garden, which was already being called Covent Garden, he entertained an exclusive circle of friends, which soon included Kit. These men were the free-thinkers of late Elizabethan times. They called themselves 'The School of Night', and under their gentle, wise master, Thomas Harriott, the astronomer and mathematician, they met regularly to study problems of philosophy, theology, astronomy, geography and chemistry. They were the first of many similar groups of intellectuals who, a century or more later, were to make Covent Garden the centre of London's literary and artistic life.

The broadsheets abused The School of Night unmercifully. When Harriott made it known that he considered the resurrection of the body and the creation of the world in seven days as physical impossibilities, they called him the devil incarnate. They accused the school of practising black magic and alchemy. 'Black devils' one broadsheet called them, and added: 'The members of the School of Night indulge in the disgusting habit of tobacco smoking. A silver pipe is passed from man to man round the table, when they are in session. Their stomachs are therefore as black with soot as their hearts and minds with evil.'

Kit, who only a few years later was to meet a violent and tragic death, was fascinated by the twilight world of necromancy, and his work showed the anguish of so many Elizabethan intellectuals, desperately floundering through the mists of medieval superstition to find the world of truth.

As late as 1627 there were still only two people rated to the parish of St Martin-in-the-Fields under Covent Garden, but the population of London was still growing rapidly. At the beginning of Queen Elizabeth's reign it was about fifty thousand in the City, with another twenty thousand living outside the walls, and by the beginning of the seventeenth century it had doubled itself.

Cheapside had become a fine, wide street, and the steeply roofed houses of the wealthy citizens were now built of brick and elaborately carved timber, with sometimes four or five overhanging storeys, so that the top floors on opposite sides of the street nearly met, and often there was a balcony on the second or third floor; but the appallingly overcrowded dwellings of the artisans, still built of wood and plaster, were as primitive as ever, run up quickly, wherever space could be found for them.

In 1580 Queen Elizabeth issued a proclamation forbidding the creation of any but houses of the highest class within three miles of the City. The Stuarts were even more concerned, for the population of London was now approaching 200,000. In 1617 James I commanded all noblemen, knights and gentlemen who had mansions in the country to depart within twenty days, with their wives and families, during the summer vacation.

This was the year that the London apprentices destroyed the Cockpit in Drury Lane, but it was soon rebuilt.

Elements of classical architecture were appearing in the traditional Gothic of English architecture by this time, but now came the great change. Inigo Jones was a Londoner, born in Smithfield in 1571, the son of a cloth worker. Little is known of his early years, but from boyhood he was interested in painting and architecture and the 'arts of design', and when he was in his early twenties he undertook a journey to Italy to study its buildings – old and new – and their decoration. He visited Venice, Rome and Florence and made a careful study of the laws of symmetry and proportion which Palladio had evolved from his study of ancient buildings. Inigo Jones came to the notice of Princess Anne of Denmark, the bride of James VI of

Scotland; and when, in 1603, he succeeded to the English throne as James I and they arrived in England she sent for Inigo, to design the masques that had become so popular at Court, which involved contriving the scenery, the stage effects and the costumes, while Ben Jonson did most of the writing.

Not until 1615 was Inigo Jones appointed Surveyor of His Majesty's Works, and then he introduced the first true Renaissance dwelling in the country, with his design for the Queen's House at Greenwich, which was a purely Italian villa, with a flat parapet which hid the roof and had its principal rooms on the first floor. Nothing like it had ever been seen before in England, and it was to have a profound influence on English domestic building. He continued designing masques for the Court, and when, in 1619, the banqueting hall at the Whitehall Palace, which had already replaced a wooden one, was burnt down, he designed the third, which stands to this day, being now the Royal United Services Museum.

He was then asked to lay out the Lincoln's Inn fields and build a chapel there, it having been decided that 'fair and goodly walks would be a matter of great ornament to the City', as well as providing 'pleasure and freshness for the health and recreation of the inhabitants thereabouts'. He was given permission to clear away the few existing houses, after compensation was paid to the owners, and set to work, but it was left to others to complete the task for he was a busy man and had been called away to begin the restoration of old St Paul's.

When Charles I came to the throne, in 1625, he made a determined effort to check the haphazard building in London, for still people felt that they had the right to build what they liked, wherever they could find the space, without any consideration either for their neighbours or for the general public.

He went so far as to forbid the entertainment of additional inmates in houses already existing, 'which would multiply the inhabitants to such an excessive number that they could neither be governed nor fed', a decree which by no means endeared him to his subjects. No new building on new foundations was to be built within two miles of London, and henceforth, for safety and endurance, all houses were to be built of brick and the overhanging storeys of the earlier days, always a fire hazard, were forbidden.

He appointed a commission to see that these orders were obeyed, and amongst its fifty members was Inigo Jones, on whom most of the practical work devolved. The commission had to report what houses, buildings and streets were being built in any other way than that directed and had the power to commit to prison any owners and workmen who presumed to proceed with a building after being ordered to stop.

Twenty houses which had been built speculatively in St Martin's Lane had to be demolished. Sir Kenelm Digby planned to put up some houses on an open space near Drury Lane, but he was refused permission, and the commission reported that various people who had attempted to build on the site had been committed to Newgate 'until they had demolished them' and that the site was intended for the 'planting of trees and for pleasant and wholesome walks for the commoditie of the inhabitants'.

Yet building went on, and the more prosperous were soon exchanging the threat of demolition for the payment of a fine.

It was at this stage that at last the Russell family decided to lay out their inheritance of the convent garden as a building site. The Earl was given official permission by the King, who, on 10 January 1631, ordered the Attorney-General to prepare a licence to Francis, Earl of Bedford. The Earl then asked Inigo Jones to design a square surrounded by noble mansions, with four streets to converge on it.

Inigo planned an Italian piazza, five hundred feet long and four hundred feet wide, surrounded by tall houses whose first floors projected over the pavement and were supported by plaster-covered brick pillars to form arcades. The vegetable plots and ancient fruit trees all disappeared, and the builders set to work. Londoners were entranced by the novelty of the piazza and the arcades, which they also called 'piazzas': they have been called the piazzas ever since. The houses of the northern and eastern piazzas took shape, tall and spacious, with pediments and pilasters. The interiors had elegant staircases and beautifully proportioned rooms, many in the form of a double cube, with friezes and panels of moulding, ceilings of Italian plaster work and marble floors. But the southern piazza was never built, and the boundary of the square on this side remained the tree-shaded garden wall of Bedford House, while on the western side the Russells decided to build a small chapel. For Inigo Jones it was a sadly missed opportunity, for his original conception of the piazza would have been very beautiful; but the Russell family funds were running low, and the story goes that when the Earl sent for Inigo to discuss the building of the chapel, he told him that it must not cost too much. 'In short,' he said, 'I would have it not much better than a barn.' 'Well, then,' said Inigo, 'you shall have the handsomest barn in England.'

Work began in 1631, with the beautiful Tuscan portico facing eastwards on to the piazza, but then the Bishop, William Laud, insisted that the altar should be against the east wall, so the portico was closed and never used, two small entrances being made on either side of it. The main entrance was by the big west door, opening onto the little graveyard leading to the country lane which was soon to become Bedford Street. The church was completed in 1633, costing the Russells only £4,500, but it was not dedicated until 1638.

The market people did not move. They assembled their wares under the garden wall of Bedford House, and business flourished, for people flocked to watch the piazza taking shape and there were now scores of workmen about – bricklayers, carpenters, glaziers and plasterers – as additional customers.

Once the houses were completed, the Russell family had no trouble in finding tenants, for the wealthy were delighted with the new Palladian houses, so close to both the City and Westminster, and Covent Garden became fashionable and exclusive.

The building of the four streets leading to the square was soon under way. King Street, north of the piazza, ran from east to west; Henrietta Street, named after King Charles's queen, was parallel to King Street, to the south, both of them leading from Bedford Street. James Street, named after the Duke of York, who was to become the luckless James II, ran from the middle of King Street northwards to Long Acre, where already the avenue of elm trees had been felled, to make way for new houses. Russell Street ran from the middle of the eastern piazza eastwards, cutting across yet another new street, Bow Street, 'being so built as running in the shape of a bent bow', which ran on to Long Acre, while Russell Street was continued to Drury Lane. The houses in these streets were smaller than those of the piazzas, but beautifully appointed, with interesting staircases and carved panelling, and they were all elegant and fashionable in these early years.

Yet they were still having trouble with the speculative builders who had previously leased land from the Russells. The Earl of Clare, who had built a house to the east of Drury Lane, was complaining, in 1638, that two stables adjoining his garden had been illegally turned into dwelling-houses, with chimneys which smoked across his garden and gallery. In the same year, John Ward began building some small houses on land lying between the northern piazza and Long Acre. He planned to build seventeen of these cottages, each with two rooms down and two up and a small backyard; and on the assumption that Lady Stanhope, now living in the northern piazza, would lease him some of her land, he had designed a narrow, covered alley which would give the cottages access to the new square.

Inigo Jones and the Commission saw this plan as the making of a slum, and after three months they stopped the work, and the half-built cottages were demolished.

By the end of the 1630s the eastern side of St Martin's Lane had been built as far as Long Acre, extending at this time southwards to the Strand. Charles Street, King William Street, Bedfordbury, New Street, Chandos Street and Maiden Lane were all established.

By 1645 the Bedford development had become so populous and so many new streets were being built, including, just beyond its boundaries, Great Queen Street and Little Queen Street, that, despite the protests of the incumbent of St Martin-in-the-Fields, Covent Garden was made into a separate parish and Inigo Jones's little church was dedicated to St Paul.

2

First Theatres and Families

In Covent Garden very little has survived of the work of Inigo Jones and his nephew-in-law, the young John Webb, who was now his assistant; but the beautiful façade of the house in the north-west corner, adjoining King Street, and now known as 43 King Street, still survives. Its first occupant was the Earl of Stirling, who died in 1640, and the second was Thomas Killigrew, a page in the household of Charles I and companion in exile of Charles II, who was to play so important a part in the story of Covent Garden after the Restoration.

In 1644 Denzil Holles, one of the five members who defied King Charles in the days leading up to the Civil War, was living in this house for two or three years, and then Sir Harry Vane, who was also to side with the Parliamentary forces; although he later quarrelled with Cromwell and his military dictatorship, and refused to take part in the trial of King Charles, at the Restoration he was nevertheless included in the list of regicides and executed on Tower Hill.

Wentworth, Lord Strafford, whose execution in 1641 was to be a grief to Charles I for the rest of the few years left to him, had a house on the south side of Henrietta Street, while Cromwell himself lived in Long Acre from 1637 till 1643, and in 1646, after his victories at Marston Moor and Naseby, he had a lodging in Bow Street.

In 1634 Sir Edmund Verney rented, for £160 a year, two houses in the northern part of the eastern piazza, at the corner of Russell Street, where later the Bedford Coffee House was to be established; but, like Strafford, he was not to enjoy his London home for long, for during the Civil War he was King Charles's standard-bearer and met his death at Edgehill.

In the Verney papers there is a list of the coach-houses and stables that went with the property, and they state that the principal apartments of the houses had 'shuttynge windows' and that the door of almost every room had its 'stocklock'. Although Sir Edmund could not regard the portico walk in front of his houses as part of the rented property, he was given the right 'to expel youths playing in the said walk to his offence and disturbance'. Even more important, since there was as yet no sewer serving the square, Sir Edmund insisted on a clause in the lease that 'if he should be annoyed by that circumstance as not to be able to continue there with any conveyancy', he might resign his occupancy, on giving six months notice.

The Marquis of Winchester, the Countess of Peterborough, Sir John Wittwing, Lord Wilmot and the Earl of Sussex were other residents in the square before the Civil War, while Inigo Jones built himself a house in St Martin's Lane.

For the mercers and merchants, wig-makers and tailors, printers and bookbinders, bakers and butchers, who now crowded in to serve the wealthy residents, shops were opened in the side streets; and for the artisans and the very poor, small places were built in the developing little courts and alleyways, the landlords often compensating themselves for the fines imposed on them by charging higher rents, but within a few years many of these courtyards, particularly those off Drury Lane, had degenerated into slums. Phoenix Alley – now called Hanover Place – was built in 1637, and here John Taylor, the Thames waterman who became known as the Water Poet, kept his tavern 'The Crown'. At a small street off Drury Lane, with the unfortunate name of Dirty Lane, John Aubrey wrote his *Brief Lives*. Edmund Waller, a cousin of John Hampden, had his London home in Bow Street; much of his poetry, including 'Go, lovely Rose!' was dedicated to the great love of his life, Lady Dorothea Sidney, who nevertheless rejected him for the Earl of Sunderland. New Row, running from St Martin's Lane to King Street, was built in 1644 by the first Duke of Bedford, on the site of Castel Alley and Sunne Alley, and consisted mostly of small shops, but there was one stately home there – on the site of Number 14 – the house of the Countess of Chesterfield, who was loved and painted by Charles I's Court painter, Van Dyck.

There was a plentiful supply of beerhouses and taverns, and as well as the Cockpit theatre in Drury Lane there was another in Vere Street, lying between Drury Lane and Lincoln's Inn Fields, close to Clare market, which the Earl of Clare had opened for the sale of fish and meat.

In Drury Lane, about where Wild Street joins it, the Wild family of Lulworth Castle had built their London home, Wild House, and it was here that Walter Butler, heir to the Earl of Ormonde, came to live in 1625, after eleven years in the Fleet prison, to which he had been consigned by James I.

It had been a disgraceful affair. James I, short of money and with a large following of Scottish nobles, all of whom were expecting handsome livings, had insisted, on the promptings of his beloved George Villiers, that the Earl's widowed daughter, Elizabeth, be married to Sir Richard Preston, who was in sore need of a rich wife, since no profitable Court office had yet come his way. And when, shortly afterwards, the old Earl of Ormonde died, leaving Walter Butler heir to Kilkenny and all the Ormonde estates, Preston queried the inheritance and insisted that, as Elizabeth's husband, it should come to him. After two or three years' litigation, King James, anxious to break the power of the Catholic Ormondes in Ireland, informed Walter that he had decided that the castle of Kilkenny and the estates attached to it should go to Preston, now created Lord Dingwall. Walter, refusing to accept so outrageous a decision, was fined £100,000, but, sooner than impoverish his family, he refused to pay and was sent to the Fleet prison, only to be released on the death of James and the accession of Charles I, who granted him £1,000 a year from his Irish rents but decreed that the remainder should be kept in the hands of the trustees appointed by the Crown, until the fine had been paid.

Walter's only son, John, came from Ireland to visit his father in prison, but on the way the boat foundered off the treacherous Skerries and there was not a single survivor. John's son, the nine-year-old James, had been sent to a Roman Catholic seminary at Finchley, but King James now made him a ward of Court and had him moved to Lambeth Palace, to be brought up as a Protestant under Archbishop Abbot. And it was not until his grandfather, Sir Walter, had established himself in Drury Lane that James was allowed out of Lambeth Palace, for the first time in six years, to visit him. But for another two years he had to continue living at Lambeth, so it was not until 1627, when he was seventeen, that he was free to join Sir Walter at Wild House, to explore the City, visit the theatres, establish himself at Court and, within a few years, watch the building of the Covent Garden piazza.

On the north side of Russell Street lived Robert Carr, Earl of Somerset, who had survived the Overbury scandal of King James's reign by thirty years, and died there in 1645, being one of the first to be buried in the graveyard of St Paul's Church.

The trouble had begun in 1607, when the beautiful little Frances Howard was married, at the age of thirteen, to the fourteen-year-old Earl of Essex. After the wedding festivities, the bride was sent home to her parents for a few years, and the young Earl was sent abroad to finish his education. But soon Frances had fallen in love with Robert Carr, the handsome young man who had supplanted Philip Herbert in King James's affections. Not unnaturally, Carr was hated by the Queen, and to complicate matters, it was at this point that the Earl of Essex returned to England to claim his bride. Frances took a violent dislike to him and refused to consummate the marriage. She turned to her great-uncle, the Earl of Northampton, for help, and he in his turn sent for Anne Turner, to comfort and advise his favourite niece. She was the young woman who helped Inigo Jones with his costumes, and had become indispensable not only to him but also to the ladies of the Court, being their willing confidant and adviser and often giving them love potions and similar aphrodisiacs of her own brewing, to help the course of their love affairs.

The question of the annulment of the Essex marriage was discussed. Thomas Overbury, one of Carr's oldest friends, supported the Queen, probably for political reasons, and did all he could to prevent it. To silence him, he was committed to the Tower on a trumped-up charge, but Frances, still afraid of the harm he could do, for he alone knew of her brief affair with Prince Henry, who had recently died, at the age of eighteen, turned again to Anne Turner.

Pocketing a handsome fee, Anne reassured her that all would be well in the end. Overbury became very ill. Doctors attended him in the Tower, but in vain. A few days later, he died in agony, with all the symptoms of poisoning.

Archbishop Abbot still refused to annul the Essex marriage, but a few weeks later King James commanded him to do so with no more delay – on the alleged grounds of the Earl's impotency – and as it had become extremely inadvisable to oppose the King's wishes, the unhappy Archbishop, anxious to retain his office, felt that he had no option but to obey. So Carr was created Earl of Somerset and Frances became the Countess, the King presenting her with £10,000 of jewellery as a wedding gift, although some of his servants had not been paid for months.

George Villiers now supplanted Carr in the King's affections and began a whispering campaign of suspicion which quickly became too strong to be ignored. In October 1614 Anne Turner and her servant were arrested and brought to trial. In the end, Anne confessed to having sent poisoned food to Overbury in the Tower and was condemned to be hanged at Tyburn. Then both Frances and her husband were arrested and brought to trial at Westminster Hall. Somerset denied all knowledge of the plot, but Frances eventually confessed, and both were consigned to the Tower for the next six years, when the King at last set them free. Robert never forgave Frances, and they ended up by hating each other. Frances died soon afterwards of cancer, but Robert Carr, the Earl of Somerset, lived on until 1643. His daughters had married into the Bedford family, but Carr lived alone in Russell Street, disgraced and shunned, while she lived close at hand in Bedford House.

Lucy Walter was born in 1630, the same year as Charles II. She was the daughter of William Walter of Roche Castle, Pembrokeshire, a member of a distinguished family with a long line of noble ancestors. Her parents quarrelled, and when Lucy was eight years old, her father took his wife and the children to King Street, Covent Garden, near where a number of her relations and close friends were living, including her own mother, Mrs Protheroe, sister of the first Earl of Carbery and a member of the social circle associated with the Court: and here William Walter left them, returning alone to Roche Castle. So it was in Covent Garden that Lucy grew up, her girlhood friends being the Protheroes, the Howards, the Sidneys and the family of Algernon Percy, Earl of Northumberland; and it is more than probable that during these years she met Prince Charles himself.

Her father was an ardent Royalist and, with his wife's cousin, the Earl of Carbery, defended Roche Castle until, in 1644, they were forced to surrender it to the Parliament army.

King Charles was in desperate need of more troops, and while he was at Oxford, one of the many Royalists who came to him with plans for help was Lord Herbert, whom the King created the Earl of Glamorgan. However his plan miscarried and the King ordered Glamorgan to Prince Charles's Court in Paris, probably to take him some much-needed money. With him Glamorgan took his old friend John Barlow, Lucy Walter's uncle, and also Lucy herself. Why he took her no one will ever know. It may have been at the express wish of the Prince, who had already fallen in love with her in the Covent

Garden days. It has even been suggested that they had already been secretly married.

The year was 1648 and they were both eighteen. He took her to The Hague, and Lucy soon became pregnant. Their son James, the future Duke of Monmouth, was born at Rotterdam on 9 April 1649, ten weeks after the execution of King Charles I.

The following June, Prince Charles was summoned to Scotland, where he had been proclaimed King Charles II, but after the disastrous Battle of Worcester, on 3 September 1651, he escaped back to exile on the Continent. Four months earlier, Lucy had given birth to a daughter, Mary. The story spread that she had been having an intrigue with Henry Bennet, Lord Arlington. Charles refused to have any more to do with her, strongly denying that they had ever been married, despite Lucy's protestations and pleadings and her declaration that she had documents to prove that the marriage had taken place.

If it had, then her son was now the heir to the English throne. It has been suggested that Charles, being at heart a Roman Catholic, may have considered a Protestant marriage – if indeed there ever had been one – was invalid. Or perhaps, like the Duke of York's first marriage, to Anne, the daughter of Lord Clarendon, he felt that, for reasons of state, it would be better to ignore it, although it was he who was to persuade his brother not to desert Anne when she was pregnant.

Charles's sister Mary, married to the Prince of Orange, granted Lucy an annuity for a time. Her parents were both dead by now, and in 1656 she paid a visit to England, to recover a sum of £1,500 which her mother had left her. With her maid, Ann Hill, and the two children, she took lodgings over a barber's shop in the Strand, close to Somerset House, and here she lived very quietly, secretly visited by her Royalist friends still living in Covent Garden, who treated her with all the honour and deference paid to a queen. But very soon she was discovered, betrayed possibly by Tom Howard, who had accompanied her from The Hague, no one having the slightest idea that he was, in fact, a Cromwellian spy.

One morning the guards came to the lodgings over the baker's shop, and Lucy, the children and the maid were all taken to the Tower. The charge against her was never clear. Vaguely she was described as a woman of ill repute and suspected of espionage, but when nothing could be proved against her, she was released and told to leave the country immediately; afterwards she said that it was while she was in the Tower that the documents proving her marriage to Charles had been stolen from her.

They returned to Brussels, by now almost penniless, but still Charles would not see her. However, through the offices of James Ormonde, now in exile with the King and one of his closest friends, she at last agreed to hand over the little boy, whom Charles sincerely wanted to claim as his own. She made her way to Paris, where less than a year later she died, while the future Duke of Monmouth, for whom his father was now too poor to provide a proper tutor and attendants, was being cared for by his grandmother, Queen Henrietta Maria, at the Palais Royale. There is no record of what happened to the small Mary at this time, but she appears again in the Covent Garden story some years later.

The Cockpit theatre had been rebuilt after the apprentices' attack in 1617, and John Evelyn, on a visit to London from Paris, recorded that on 5 February 1647 he saw a tragi-comedy acted in the Cockpit, after there had been none of these diversions for many years during the war, but this was the year when an Act was passed for the suppression of play-acting, and the theatre became a school for a time. During the eleven years of the Commonwealth all the theatres were closed and most of them demolished, but this was the kind of law which people who felt so inclined could usually manage to evade.

By 1656 the school had failed and the Cockpit was standing empty. William Davenant, godson of Shakespeare and, some would have it, his natural son, surreptitiously began staging plays there, although at considerable risk both to the players and to the audience. On at least one occasion, soldiers broke in, cleared the auditorium, broke up the seats and the stage, confiscated the props and costumes and locked up the players for a few days. After a suitable interval, however, the company came together again, and it was here that young Thomas Betterton received his early training and the handsome young Edward Kynaston continued the tradition of boys playing women's parts, making, Pepys said, 'the loveliest lady that ever I saw in my life!'.

John Evelyn was visiting Covent Garden a good deal during the last years of the Commonwealth, for his brother was living there. On Christmas Day 1657 he came up from Deptford with his wife to celebrate Christmas, and they attended morning service at the chapel at Exeter House. Suddenly it was surrounded by soldiers, and as the congregation went up to receive the Sacrament after the sermon, the men 'held their muskets against them, as if they would have shot them at the altar: but allowed them to finish, not being sure what in fact to do in such circumstances'. All the congregation and communicants were held prisoner for a time. Evelyn and his wife, with several others, were held in one room for several hours and later examined by officers from Whitehall. Evelyn was asked why, contrary to the ordinance that had been made, they observed the superstitious time of the Nativity – and why he should be at common prayers – which were only the Mass in English – praying for Charles Stuart. Evelyn replied that they prayed for all Christian kings, princes and governors, and at last he was dismissed, 'with much pity of my ignorance'.

Little did the soldiers know what had happened to the statue of Charles I, which had stood in Whitehall. At the time of his execution it was taken down and handed over to a brazier named Rivett, to be destroyed, but he managed to hide it in the vaults of St Paul's Church. In order to give the impression that he had melted it down, he made a number of small bronze figures and vases, which he sold as relics of the statue, and after the Restoration he produced the statue intact and it was placed once more in Whitehall.

The piazza and its surrounding houses were still high fashion during the Commonwealth, and it is interesting to read that in 1657 William, the fifth Earl of Bedford, and his brothers John and Edward were granted a rebate of £7,000 on the fines which had been imposed on them for building in defiance of the proclamations of the Stuart kings, because of the great expense which the family had incurred in the building of the chapel and the improvement of the neighbourhood.

These fines were presumably for building additional to that for which Charles I had given his original permission.

But the Garden had its tragedies. The following year, in 1658, Richard Lovelace, the Cavalier poet, died penniless and alone, in a cellar in Long Acre. Born of a wealthy family, he was, said Aubrey, 'one of the handsomest men in England'. He had been chosen by the County of Kent to deliver a petition to the Long Parliament begging for the King to be restored to his rights, but was thrown into prison for his presumption, and here he wrote his poetry, perhaps the best known of all lines being, 'Stone walls do not a prison make.' He was released on £20,000 bail and went to France for a year or two, but on returning to England he was sent to prison again; when he was eventually set free, he was penniless and consumptive and, as Anthony à Wood relates, 'became very poor in body and purse, was the object of charity, went in ragged clothes (whereas when he was in his glory he wore cloth of gold and silver), and mostly lodged in obscure and dirty places, in one of which he died'.

The Royalist Ormonde family were more fortunate, although they too had to forfeit their wealth. Lady Ormonde, living in exile in Normandy, at last became so desperate for money that she came over to England with her children and sought a personal interview with Cromwell to ask for a restoration of her own private fortunes, part of which he granted her. So she was living in Wild House in Drury Lane at this time, while awaiting permission to return to Ireland, to see what was left of their estates at Dunmore and Kilkenny.

During the last years before the Restoration, the secret society of Royalists in England – the Sealed Knot – were making desperate but abortive efforts to secure the Restoration, but they were disorganized and bedevilled by spies in their midst. At last, after one particularly disappointing failure, James Ormonde told King Charles that he would go to London in disguise, to find out the real strength of their supporters. It was a highly dangerous venture but, travelling entirely alone, he reached London safely, and after making contact with one of the moving spirits of the Sealed Knot, at his lodgings in Threadneedle Street, he was directed to the home of a Roman Catholic doctor in Drury Lane for his lodging. There were a number of Roman Catholics living in this part of Covent Garden, and as early as 1628 a member of the House of Commons had declared that 'in Drury Lane for every Protestant family there were three Papist – insomuch that it may well be called Little Rome'. The doctor's house was only a few yards from the closed Cockpit theatre and the silent and shuttered Wild House, for Elizabeth, knowing nothing of her husband's secret visit, had gone to Ireland for a few weeks.

James stayed in Drury Lane for two weeks, without being discovered, and most of the meetings of the Sealed Knot he attended were held on the other side of the piazza, in Bedford Street. Then he began to suspect that one of their members, Willis, was a Commonwealth spy. Walking down Drury Lane, a day or two later, he had a sudden conviction that he was being followed. At the corner of the Lane and Long Acre was the Magpie Inn, and knowing that it had two entrances, he turned into it and ordered a tankard of ale, choosing a bench close to the Long Acre door. As he expected, within a few moments, his pursuer entered through the Drury Lane door, and James recognized him as Willis's servant. The man glanced round, obviously saw James, though he gave not a flicker of recognition, went up to the bar and ordered a drink; while his back was turned, James slipped out of the Long Acre door and doubled back the way he had come. But from the shelter of a pillared doorway he waited for a moment and saw the servant emerge from the Drury Lane door and make his way towards the doctor's house, signalling to two soldiers, waiting in a nearby doorway, to join him.

James just had time to warn the other members of the Sealed Knot of Willis's treachery before making the hazardous journey back to Cologne, with the disheartening news for the King that the plans of the Sealed Knot were still far too vague and impractical and that they were being closely watched.

What none of them knew was that Cromwell was ill. On the night of 1 September 1658 there was a violent storm of rain and thunder in England. It was the worst storm in living memory, and as trees were uprooted, chimney stacks crashed to the ground and rooftops were blown clean away, people said it was a portent of even more momentous events.

Cromwell, exhausted and disappointed with his brief experiment as Lord Protector of the Realm, took to his bed. He was still willing, he said, to live and toil, but he was also willing to die and be at rest. And on 3 September, two days after that terrible storm, he died.

During Richard Cromwell's short term as Lord Protector, the Royalists, taking advantage of the disarray of Parliament and the army, again began to make plans.

The mood of the country was changing and there was already a reaction, particularly amongst the young, against the restrictions that the Puritans had tried to impose. The mad young drinking lords were 'living very high'. They were 'frequenting taverns, cock-fighting and illicit performances at the Cockpit at Drury Lane, or the Red Bull in St John's Street'. Clarendon declared that girls 'conversed without any circumspection or modesty and frequently met at taverns or common eating houses', while as early as 1654 John Evelyn had observed 'how the women began to paint themselves, formerly a most ignominious thing, and used only by prostitutes'.

Richard Cromwell was dismissed from office, the Protectorate came to an end, and Charles was recalled to the throne.

Landing at Dover, the illustrious cavalcade journeyed by way of Canterbury and Rochester to London, where they arrived on 29 May 1660, the King's thirtieth birthday, and every mile of the route was lined with cheering, excited crowds. At Temple Bar the City companies, in their gorgeous liveries, joined the procession, as it wound its way along the Strand, to join the throng of nobles and gentry already assembled in St Paul's Cathedral for the service of thanksgiving; and all through the City the streets were hung with flags and tapestries, while from the flower-decked balconies and windows, the women and children looked down in rapture.

Amongst the watching crowds in the Strand must almost certainly have been a ten-year-old girl, Nell Gwynne, who had been born in the Coal Yard, a squalid little alley at the northern, unfashionable end of Drury Lane, where it joined Holborn.

After the service at St Paul's, the procession took seven long hours to return through the City, and it was not until nine o'clock in the evening that the tired King reached Whitehall, to receive his formal greeting from Parliament. When it was all over, he remarked wryly to James Ormonde that it must have been his own fault that he had stayed away so long, for so far he had met nobody who had not protested that he had always prayed for his return.

Ormonde was at last free to hurry back to Drury Lane for a joyful reunion at Wild House with his wife and children, after a separation of eight weary years. Not far away, Nell, in her sordid little home in the Coal Yard, slept peacefully, after the best free show she had ever known in her short life, little dreaming what the future held for her.

The market people were kept busy during these days, in their stalls and sheds under the wall of Bedford House, although it was still an informal affair and not yet licensed: but as the population of Covent Garden increased, so did the market.

3

'Sweet Nell of Old Drury'

With the Restoration, Killigrew and Davenant were soon talking to the King about the possibility of opening new theatres in London, and after much discussion they were granted a royal charter which gave them each a licence to build a theatre and employ companies of actors. The patent stated that, 'we do likewise permit and give leave that all women's parts, to be acted in either of the said Companies for the time to come, may be performed by women so long as these recreations which, by reason of the abuses aforesaid were scandalous and offensive, may by such reformation be esteemed not only harmless delights but useful and instructive representations of human life to such of our good subjects as shall resort to the same.'

At first Killigrew and Davenant ran the old Cockpit theatre* together, but soon they parted. Davenant, taking Betterton with him, went to Lincoln's Inn, where the old Clare market theatre was restored and later converted into the Duke's Theatre, named after the Duke of York, while Killigrew leased a site from the Duke of Bedford which lay at the corner of Drury Lane and Russell Street and raised the money to build the first Theatre Royal. He collected his company of actors and actresses, who became members of His Majesty's Company of Comedians in Drury Lane and, as members of the King's household, took an oath of allegiance to the King and were entitled to wear his special livery.

The greatest problem confronting the new threatre managers was what plays to present, for no one had been writing for the theatre for at least a decade, and there was no law of copyright in the plays that were available. The King therefore suggested that Davenant and Killigrew should divide between them the plays that were already in existence. Thus half of Shakespeare's and Ben Jonson's plays went to

* Sometimes known as the Phoenix.

the Duke's Theatre and half to the Theatre Royal, but Killigrew managed to acquire all the works of Beaumont and Fletcher as well.

At the Duke's Theatre, Davenant opened in 1661 with his own play *The Siege of Rhodes*, his principal players being Thomas Betterton, Mary Saunderson, whom he later married, Moll Davis and Mrs Barry. Pepys was there in September with his wife, and they were seated 'close to the King, and the Duke of York ... And here was "Bartholomew Fayre", the puppet-show, acted today, which has not been this forty years (it being so satyricall against Puritanism, they durst not till now, which is strange they should already dare to do it, and the King do countenance it) ... '

Killigrew opened at Drury Lane in May 1663, with Beaumont and Fletcher's *The Humorous Lieutenant*, which Pepys thought 'a silly play' but which pleased the audience well enough; and in the company were Charles Hart, a grand-nephew of Shakespeare, Lacy, Michael Mohun and Edward Kynaston, all of whom were talented and popular, the new leading ladies being the Marshall sisters, Anne and Beck, and Mary Knipp, of whom Pepys became so fond.

The theatre was elegant but small, holding about seven hundred people. It had two tiers of boxes, including the splendid royal box, and a gallery. The floor of the theatre was occupied by a steeply ramped pit. There was a proscenium arch framing the stage but a considerable projection of apron stage into the auditorium, as in the old Elizabethan theatre. There were windows, for the first performances were still held in daylight, but the stage was lit by candles suspended in chandeliers from the proscenium arch. Two generations later the first floats were used. There was a curtain and elaborately painted floats for scenery, but there was very little stage furniture, so that actors and actresses still tended to step forward onto the apron and declaim their parts, with the old formal gestures of the Elizabethans, who had been trained by their employers, the actor managers, to express certain emotions only by definite, appropriate gestures of the arms, hands and head.

'The house is made with extraordinary good convenience,' said Pepys, 'and yet hath some faults, as the narrowness of the passages in and out of the pit, and the distance from the stage to the boxes, which I am confident cannot hear; but for all other things is well; only, above all, the musique being below, and most of it sounding under the very stage, there is no hearing of the basses at all, nor very well of the trebles, which sure must be mended. The play was "*The*

Humorous Lieutenant", a play that hath good in it, nor much in the very part which by the King's command, Lacy now acts instead of Clun ... The play being done, we home by water, having been a little shamed that my wife and woman were in such a pickle, all the ladies being finer and better dressed in the pitt than they used, I think, to be.'

Nell Gwynne was now thirteen. Her father had died while she was still a baby. He had been a fruit-seller in the market, but it was said that he came from a landed Welsh family and had lost everything when fighting as a Captain in the Royalist armies during the Civil War, and that his ruin had been hastened by his marriage to a lowly young woman, whose only claim to fame was her addiction to brandy. He died young, leaving his widow and two little girls, Rose and Nell, destitute, and Nell, from the time she was eleven or twelve, was hawking fish and vegetables around Covent Garden. A year or two later, she became a servant to Madam Ross, who kept her brothel in Lewknor's Lane, which is now called Macklin Street, lying between Holborn and Great Queen Street.

What was happening to Rose no one knows, but the next firm news of her was that she had been committed to Newgate prison, probably for petty theft. Surprisingly, it was to Tom Killigrew that she wrote, begging him to secure her a reprieve, which he did, and shortly afterwards, still in her teens, she married John Cassells, who earned a precarious living as a highwayman. How close Rose's relationship with Killigrew had been one can only guess, but it was probably through her that Nell was able to leave Madam Ross and work at the Drury Lane theatre, selling oranges at sixpence a time, under the direction of Orange Moll, the supervisor of the young orange-sellers.

Nell was exceptionally pretty and charming, and the story goes that one of the regular theatre-goers, having noticed her looks and her intelligence, mentioned to Hart and Lacy that he thought she was wasted as an orange-seller and would probably be successful as a player. They made a point of talking to her and agreed that she had great possibilities. Lacy taught her stage dancing, and Hart gave her a few lessons in speech and deportment, and in 1665, when she was only fifteen, they decided that she was ready for her first part.

The young John Dryden had now made his name as a poet of rare distinction and was beginning to write his early, rather ponderous plays, and Nell's first appearance on the stage was in *The Indian Emperor*, an heroic play about Cortez and Montezuma in Mexico, in which she played the leading woman's part of Cydaria opposite Hart's Cortez.

The play was written in rhymed couplets and quatrains, and Nell's first line on the stage was an aside, as she fell in love with Cortez at first sight.

> My father's gone, and yet I cannot go,
> Sure I have something lost or left behind.

It was a part singularly unsuited to Nell, who was essentially a comedian, but she acted with spirit, and the audience loved her.

Yet her first triumph was brief, for only a few weeks later, in May 1665, the plague broke out in London and all the theatres were shut. It was in Covent Garden that Pepys saw the sign of the first victims. On 7 June 1665 he wrote in his diary: 'This day, much against my will, I did in Drury Lane see two or three houses marked with a red cross upon the doors, and "Lord have mercy upon us" writ there; which was a sad sight to me, being the first of its kind that, to my remembrance I ever saw.'

The theatres were to remain shut for the next eighteen months, for this was one of the most terrible visitations of the plague that the country, and London in particular, had ever known. It was an exceptionally hot summer, and by July six thousand cases had been reported in the City. Shops closed and all who could, including many of the doctors and clergy, moved away to the country. Business came to a standstill and the docks were deserted, the labourers and craftsmen thrown out of work. In August eighteen thousand died, and in September thirty thousand.

The plague 'broke the trade of the nation and swept away about a hundred thousand souls: the greatest havoc that any plague ever made in England', wrote Burney.

The wealthy inhabitants of the Covent Garden piazzas fled, but the rector of St Paul's, Simon Patrick, stayed gallantly at his post, selflessly ministering to the sick and dying, and blessing the dead at their mass funerals. When his friends warned him of his danger and begged him to leave, he replied: 'What! Am I better than another? I must stay with my charge.' His only recorded complaint is that, while burying the dead at night, as was the order, he 'found the autumn winds prejudicial'.

After the death of Sir William Drury, Drury House had been

rebuilt and occupied by Sir William Craven, who also served Covent Garden well during the plague. He bought a field not far away – where Golden Square was to be laid out – and here he built thirty-six pest-houses as a hospital for the sufferers and a refuge for those who had nowhere else to go, giving the rest of the field as a burial ground for the thousands who died. And he frequently visited the place himself 'with the same coolness with which he had fought the battles of the Queen of Bohemia, in order to maintain order and mitigate the horrors of the scene'.

Later he gave this field in trust to the poor of the parishes of St Clement Danes, St Martin-in-the-Fields and St Paul's, Covent Garden, in case the plague should reappear; and when he later moved from Drury Lane to Bayswater, this field was exchanged for one where Craven Road and Craven Hill Gardens now stand in Bayswater.

With the colder days of autumn, the plague abated and people began to return to London. On 5 January 1666 Pepys recorded that 'the towne is full, compared with what it used to be. I mean the City end; for Covent Garden and Westminster are yet very empty of people, no Court nor gentry being there'. And a few days later, on the 19th, he wrote again: 'It is a remarkable thing how infinitely naked all that end of the towne, Covent Garden, is at this day of people; while the City is almost as full again as ever it was.'

What happened to Nell during the plague is not known, but it seems probable that Hart took her away to a place of safety somewhere in the country, for he was very fond of her at this time. It was not until the following August that Pepys, meeting Orange Moll in Drury Lane, heard that the actors and actresses at Drury Lane had already assembled for rehearsals and were preparing for the coming winter season.

Only a few days later, tragedy came again to London. Early in the morning of 2 September fire broke out in the house of the King's baker in Pudding Lane, starting a blaze which was to spread with terrifying speed through the wooden houses of the City and destroy 430 acres of London, 300 of them within the walls. The loss included more than 13,000 houses, the halls of 44 of the City companies and 89 parish churches, as well as St Paul's Cathedral, the Royal Exchange, the Customs House, part of the Guildhall and four of the City gates.

After the first stunned shock of the disaster, the rebuilding of

London was soon under way. Inigo Jones had died in 1652, during the Commonwealth, but the brilliant Christopher Wren, born in 1632, who as a young man had been professor of astronomy at Oxford but, like Inigo Jones, had become keenly interested in Italian Renaissance architecture, had been appointed the King's Surveyor. Just before the Great Fire he had actually submitted plans to Charles II for the rebuilding of Old St Paul's, which had fast been crumbling into ruin and had been further damaged by Cromwell's troops during the Commonwealth, but now the old place had gone for ever.

While Wren began his enormous task of replanning the City of London, a plan which, sadly, was never to be properly fulfilled, there was a new exodus from the ruined City westwards to Covent Garden.

The Puritans declared that the plague and the terrible fire, together with the reverses and humiliations which the country was suffering in the Dutch wars, were God's punishment for the evil ways of the people, and in particular the licentiousness of the Restoration Court and the theatres. Nevertheless, the theatres re-opened and Nell was back at Drury Lane. In December Pepys was enjoying a play by James Howard, brother-in-law of Dryden, called *The English Monsieur*, a comedy in which Nell came into her own, Pepys recording: 'A mighty pretty play, very witty and pleasant. And the women do very well; but above all little Nelly ... '

She was now living in the fashionable Covent Garden end of Drury Lane, near the gates of Craven House and in view of the re-erected maypole in the Strand. Pepys saw her there a few weeks later, on May Day 1667. 'Thence to Westminster; in the way meeting many milk maids with their garlands upon their pails, dancing with a fiddler before them; and saw pretty Nelly standing at her lodgings' door in Drury Lane in her smock sleeves and bodice, looking upon them; she seemed a mighty pretty creature.'

New writers were now producing a flood of dramatic material. The most notable of these Restoration dramatists, in addition to Dryden and Davenant of the first years, were John Wilson, the Earl of Orrery, Sir Robert Howard, Nathaniel Lee, Thomas Shadwell, Sir George Etherege, William Wycherley, Congreve, Thomas Otway, Sir John Vanbrugh, Mrs Aphra Benn, Mrs Centilivre, George Farquhar, the Killigrews, Sir Charles Sedley and the actor Lacy. None of them approached the genius of Shakespeare, and many of the plays were too mannered and formal. The dialogue was often brilliantly witty, but at the same time it became increasingly bawdy, often to the point of lewdness. The reaction to Puritanism had swung too far.

J. Saunders, writing in 1843, many years before Victorian prudery had developed so strongly, said that 'perhaps the most characteristic feature of the restored English theatre was its extraordinary facility for extracting evil out of everything it touched. The Elizabethan drama was not forgotten – far from it; there is scarcely a grossness in these old writers which the new ones did not now imitate and greatly improve upon; they only forgot the truth and vividness of character and life that accompanied them – their high sentiments, their noble passions, their wonderful, ever-gushing poetry ... Yet universal popularity amongst playgoers was theirs – unbounded the royal admiration and approval of their works. Theatres filled – in opposition to the puritan spirit it became a proof of loyalty to attend them ...'

Within a few weeks of the re-opening of Drury Lane, Nell had attracted the attention of the young Charles Sackville, Lord Buckhurst, and on 13 July 1667 Pepys recorded that 'my Lord Buckhurst hath got Nell away from the King's House, and gives her £100 a year ... and she will act no more'.

Buckhurst took her to Epsom which, apart from the attraction of the races, had become a fashionable spa, and he invited a friend, the notorious rake Sir Charles Sedley, to join them there, at the small house he had rented, next door to the King's Head inn.

What happened at Epsom is not clear, but the love affair ended abruptly, and only five weeks later Nell was back in London, playing again at Drury Lane. From Orange Moll, Pepys learnt that Buckhurst had left her 'and makes sport of her, and swears she hath had all she could get out of him: and Hart, her great admirer, now hates her: and that she is very poor ... and she is come to the King's House, but is neglected by them all'.

This seems out of character, for Nell was by no means avaricious. She was more interested in having a good time than accumulating money. She was careless with it and had no sense of its value. However, the management was glad to have her back, and she worked steadily for the next few months, in the plays of Beaumont and Fletcher, Dryden and Sir Robert Howard, although she was too often cast in serious parts which did not suit her, instead of the humorous roles which she did so supremely well.

On 5 October Pepys, visiting the theatre with his wife, met his beloved Knipp, who took them up to the dressing-rooms. There they found Nell dressing herself 'and was all unready, and is very pretty, prettier than I thought ... But, Lord, to see how they were both painted would make a man mad, and did make me loath them; and what base company of men comes among them, and how lewdly they talk! and how poor men are in clothes, and yet what a show they make on the stage by candle-light, is very observable. But to see how Nell curses, for having so few people in the pit, was pretty.'

On 11 November he went again to Drury Lane, and again Nell was cast in a part that did not suit her. It was once more *The Indian Emperor*, 'a good play,' said Pepys, 'but not so good as people cry it up, I think, though above all things Nell's ill speaking of a great part made me mad'. And again, on 26 December, he saw *The Surprizall*, 'which did not please me today, the actors not pleasing me; and especially Nell's acting of a serious part, which she spoils'. But two days later, when he saw her in *The Mad Couple*, he was full of praise. 'It was,' he said, 'but on ordinary play; but only Nell's and Hart's mad parts are most excellently done, but especially hers: which makes it a miracle to me to think how ill she do any serious part, as, the other day, just like a fool or changeling: and in a mad part, do beyond all imitation almost.'

King Charles now became attracted to Moll Davis, the actress and dancer at the Duke's theatre in Lincoln's Inn, but he was also becoming interested in Nell. Once more it was Pepys who tells the story. He went to Drury Lane theatre on 11 January, and Knipp came and sat with him, telling him how 'Miss Davis is for certain going away from the Duke's House, the King being in love with her; and a house is taken for her, and furnishing; and she hath a ring given her already, worth £600: that the King did send several times for Nelly, and she was with him, but what she did she knows not; this was a good while ago, and she says that the King first spoiled Mrs Weaver [another actress at the Duke of York's theatre, Lincoln's Inn] which is very mean, methinks, in a Prince; and I am sorry for it, and can hope for no good to the State from having a Prince devoted to his pleasure.'

A few days later, Pepys heard from his friend Mrs Pierce that she had recently sat near Moll Davis at the Duke's Theatre and that she was 'the most impertinent slut in the world; and the more, now the King do show her countenance; and is reckoned his mistress, even to the scorn of the whole world; the King gazing on her, and my Lady

Castlemaine (his current mistress) being melancholy and out of humour, all the play, not smiling once'.

Moll left the stage in the spring of 1668 and retired to the house in Suffolk Street that the King had given her, where her daughter was born, acknowledged by Charles as his and given the name of Mary Tudor; but by this time he was fully occupied with Nell, and left Moll, with an allowance of £1,000 a year.

All through 1668 Nell was working at Drury Lane theatre. Pepys, at the stage door to see Knipp, 'did see Beck Marshall come dressed, off the stage, and look mighty fine, and pretty, and noble; and also Nell, in her boy's clothes, mighty pretty ... but Lord! their confidence! and how many men do hover about them as soon as they come off the stage, and how confident they are in their talk'.

Nell was now a mistress of the King. In August 1669 she became pregnant and moved from her lodging in Drury Lane to Lincoln's Inn Fields for a time, and on 8 May 1670 she gave birth to her first son, Charles, the future Duke of St Albans and Earl of Burford.

Nell returned to the stage after she had recovered from her son's birth, but after a few months the King, who was genuinely and lastingly fond of her, installed her at a small house in Pall Mall, and then in a larger one, where today Number 79 stands, with a garden that overlooked that of the King; and she never returned to work at Covent Garden.

Killigrew managed to pay his way at Drury Lane, and that says a good deal for the entertainment, for his audiences were a boisterous, rowdy, critical crowd, quick to acclaim and equally prompt to shout their disapproval when they were dissatisfied. As the candle and wax lighting improved, performances took place later into the evening, although venturing out after dark was in itself a fairly hazardous undertaking, with footpads, thieves and cut-throats lurking in the dark, twisting alleys and courts around the Lane. The people poured noisily into the theatre, pitting their wits against the men at the door who took their money, and found places for themselves in the pit or gallery. Then arrived the gentry, the fops and dandies, in their curled wigs and full-skirted coats, their satin waistcoats and full breeches, preening themselves in their boxes or even on the stage itself, to be better seen.

With them came their wives and mistresses, in their long full skirts and low-cut bodices, their powdered curls and velvet cloaks, decorously masked as time went on and the Restoration plays became even bawdier and more outrageous. The masks were to hide their blushes, they said, but they also established an anonymity which at times was useful both to themselves and to their escorts.

Davenant died in 1668, and his widow and two sons planned to leave the Lincoln's Inn theatre and open a new one in Dorset Fields, down by the river, off Fleet Street. At Drury Lane, Killigrew staged Dryden, Ben Jonson and, in 1671, the Duke of Buckingham's satire *The Rehearsal*. This was the year that the Davenants opened their new theatre. It was a beautiful house, designed by Christopher Wren, with the newest ideas in lighting and stage equipment, and the company was again headed by Thomas Betterton, who was reaching the peak of his powers. People flocked to hear him, and Killigrew's audiences began to dwindle.

Betterton was undoubtedly the finest actor of his time. 'It's beyond imagination,' whispered Pepys to his companion, while watching Betterton's Hamlet. 'Mr Betterton is the best actor in the world.'

Although no one had yet thought of designing historically accurate stage costume, and players still appeared, for all parts and periods, in the current fashion of wigs, coats and breeches, with full skirts and petticoats, low bodices and long, full sleeves for the women, Betterton had developed his own acting technique since the days of his early training at the Cockpit. 'When you speak of yourself,' he said, 'the right, not the left hand, must be applied to the bosom ... but this action, generally speaking, should be only applied or expressed by laying the hand gently on the breast and not by thumping it as some people do. The gesture must pass from the left to the right and there end in gentleness and moderation.'

Betterton's style must have been a welcome contrast to the ranting performance, the strutting and roaring, of the earlier tragedians. His restraint, far from diminishing his power, enhanced it, for Barton Booth, that other distinguished actor of the Restoration theatre, acting the Ghost to Betterton's Hamlet, confessed that 'instead of aweing me, he terrified me, but divinity hung around the man'.

As the Davenants' new theatre prospered, at Drury Lane came the final disaster. In January 1672, after the play was over and everyone had gone home, fire broke out in Orange Moll's store-room and quickly spread. The brave new Theatre Royal was totally destroyed.

Tom Killigrew's first concern was for the livelihood of his company. He moved them to the old Duke's Theatre in Lincoln's Inn and then set about raising money for the rebuilding of Drury Lane.

He employed Christopher Wren to build the new Theatre Royal, which he planned to be much larger than the old one and hold some two thousand people. Again it had an apron stage, but funds were low, and the theatre had to be very plain compared with the first one. He opened in March 1674 with another play by Beaumont and Fletcher, this time *The Beggar's Bush*. The opening night was a success, but the good times did not last, and the Duke's Theatre in Dorset Fields for a long time remained more popular. As audiences grew smaller, so did the salaries of the players, and more and more of them, including Anne Marshall, deserted to the Davenants' theatre.

Killigrew and several of his original company were growing old and tired. Killigrew retired, handing his patent to his two sons, but neither Charles nor Henry Killigrew had their father's flair for the theatre. They mismanaged badly and matters went steadily downhill. They blamed the popularity of the Duke's Theatre for their misfortunes, but this was not entirely true now, for there seems to have been a bad slump early in the 1680s, and their rivals were running into trouble too. By the end of 1682 they thought they had solved the problem by amalgamating, and with Thomas Betterton as the leading actor and the Davenant brothers in management, Drury Lane seemed set for a revival of its fortunes.

The players were the most talented and distinguished that the theatre had ever had, and now the piazza and its surrounding streets, the taverns and new coffee-houses of Covent Garden were to know such great names in theatrical history as the Mountforts, the Leighs, Mrs Bracegirdle and Mrs Barry, as well as the best of the old Drury Lane company, particularly Edward Kynaston.

The fine new theatre in Dorset Fields became tarnished and neglected. It was bought by Christopher Rich but did not survive for long and was finally pulled down. Drury Lane was supreme once more, the only theatre with a royal patent.

The old names were fast disappearing. In 1682 Lacy died, and the following year both Tom Killigrew and Charles Hart. This was a great grief to Nell Gwynne, still living in her splendid house in Pall Mall, for she had never forgotten her old friends, while living a gay life of dancing and gambling with her new ones, who included the Duke of York and the beautiful young Duke of Monmouth. She engaged the almost penniless Thomas Otway, one of the best of the tragic dramatists of his time, to tutor her son Charles, and did her best to help Nathaniel Lee and Samuel Butler, the author of

Hudibras, both of whom were in dire straits. She was good to her family, too. When Rose's highwayman husband was at last caught and imprisoned, she obtained a pardon for him, and when he eventually died, she found a worthier husband for Rose, arranging what was to prove a happy and prosperous marriage. In 1679 old Mrs Gwynne died, as she had lived, in a state of drunkenness. She had visited the Neat Houses, the houses of the market gardeners which stood on the riverside at Millbank. But the Neat Houses sold drink as well as fruit and vegetables, and Mrs Gwynne, having drunk herself into a state of stupor, fell into a waterlogged ditch and drowned. Nell, though hard-pressed for money at the time, because of gambling debts, gave her a magnificent funeral at St Martin-in-the-Fields.

Despite his various aristocratic mistresses, it was with the good-tempered and sweet-natured Nell that King Charles seemed to keep on the most affectionate terms, for she made no pretence to be other than she was and never attempted to mix in politics. 'In respect of the State, I am a sleeping partner,' she said, and to Charles she was a complete relaxation.

In 1671 she had had a second son by him, but to her great sorrow he died in 1680, when he was only nine years old.

On the morning of 2 February 1685 the King was suddenly taken ill. He seemed to recover, but three days later he was dead. He had intended to create Nell, Countess of Greenwich, but he died too soon. She herself was far from well and heavily in debt. Her creditors pressed her, but the new King James was generous and did what he could to help her. She was saved from a debtors' prison but her illness grew worse. It was diagnosed as apoplexy, but it may well have been induced syphilis, contracted from the King, whose last illness had also been described as apoplexy. Only two years later, on 14 November 1687, at the age of thirty-seven, she died in her house in Pall Mall.

Nothing more had been heard of Moll Davis for a long time, but in this same year she too died, having moved from Suffolk Street to a house in the newly built St James's Square.

It was during these years that Grinling Gibbons rose to fame. John Evelyn records his discovery of the young woodcarver in January 1671, 'in an obscure place by mere accident, as I was walking near a poor solitary thatched house, in a field in our parish, near Sayes Court. I found him shut in; but looking in at a window, I perceived him carving that large cartoon, or crucifix, of Tintoretto, a copy of which I had myself brought from Venice, where the original painting remains. I asked if I might enter; he opened the door civilly to me, and I saw him about such a work as for the curiosity of handling, drawing, and studious exactness, I never had before seen in all my travels ... Of this young artist, together with my manner of finding him out, I acquainted the King, and begged that he would give me leave to bring him and his work to Whitehall, for that I would venture my reputation with his Majesty that he had never seen anything approach it, and that he would be exceedingly pleased and employ him. The King said he would himself go to see him. This was the first notice his Majesty ever had of Mr Gibbon.'

Grinling Gibbons was soon established in London, working on the carvings in the choir of the new St Paul's Cathedral, and by 1678 he was living in a house on the east side of Bow Street, called the King's Arms; here he remained until his death in 1721, except for a brief interval, recorded in the *Postman* on 24 January 1701, which ran: 'On Thursday the house of Mr Gibbons, the famous carver, in Bow Street, fell down; but by a special Providence none of the family were killed; but 'tis said that a young girl, which was playing in the court, being missing, is supposed to be buried in the rubbish.'

Why the house fell down or what happened to the small girl has never been recorded, but Gibbons and his family moved into lodgings in the piazza while their house was being rebuilt.

At the Drury Lane theatre, the Davenants proved no better managers than the Killigrew brothers had been. It was not long before they sold their patent to Christopher Rich, who was to remain at the Lane for the next ten years, despite quarrels and dissension amonst his company.

By this time, James II was in exile, and William and Mary were on the throne.

One day in 1692 there arrived at Drury Lane a young man called William Congreve. He persuaded Rich and Betterton to read a play he had just written – *The Old Bachelor* – and when they presented it, a few months later, it was a resounding success. Congreve followed it with *The Double Dealer*. And then, on a day when Kynaston was too ill to play his role of Lord Touchwood, a raw understudy, little dreaming of the heights to which fortune would one day lift him, stepped into the part. It was Colley Cibber.

But behind the scenes, resentment against Christopher Rich was growing. Salaries were not only low but irregularly paid. At last Betterton appealed to King William and obtained permission for a licence to re-open the old theatre in Lincoln's Inn. Many of his colleagues went with him, and so did the young Congreve, writing *Love for Love* for their opening night. Cibber remained with Rich, and for the next few years the rivalry between the two theatres was intense. Cibber was no great actor, but he gained his real success when he wrote and acted in his own play, *Love's Last Shift*, and when Sir John Vanbrugh wrote a sequel for it – *The Relapse* or *Virtue in Danger*, the Lane seemed to be on its feet again. Their luck held for a while, for George Farquhar wrote *Love And A Bottle* and *The Constant Couple* for them. They found another rising star in Robert Wilks, and Doggett, the popular comedian, came over to them from Lincoln's Inn.

By the end of the century, however, stagnation was descending on the English theatre. Dryden had written his last play in 1675. Wycherley had sunk into debt and was spending time in the Fleet prison, although he lived on until 1715, still in his house in Bow Street, from where he was buried at St Paul's, mourned by his new young bride of only a few days, as well as many others, for he was universally loved.

Etherege was dead. In dire poverty, despite Nell's help, poor Otway had died, when he was only thirty-three, of drink and a broken heart, from a hopeless, unrequited love for Mrs Barry. Congreve never wrote another play after *The Way of the World*, produced at Lincoln's Inn in 1700, but spent the next twenty-four years of his life basking in the honours he had won as a literary wit and enjoying life with his mistress, the Duchess of Marlborough, who, at the appointed time, gave him a truly magnificent funeral at Westminster Abbey.

In 1698 Jeremy Collier published his *Short View of the Immorality of the English Stage*, a protest against the obscenity, profanity and immorality of the plays which had been appearing on the London stage. Congreve and Vanbrugh tried to justify themselves, but Dryden admitted that 'in many things he has taxed me justly'. Most people agreed with Collier, and those who were not shocked had become unspeakably bored with them. Tastes had changed, and the plays of the Restoration years were to sink into a long oblivion.

4

The Coffee Houses

In the main square of Covent Garden seats had been placed and trees planted, and in 1658 the whole area had been gravelled and enclosed by rails. Strype, in describing it, said: 'Within the rails is a stone Pillar or Column raised on a pedestal ascended by steps, on which is placed a curious Sun-Dial, four square, having above it a mound with gilt, all neatly wrought in Freestone.'

Then, in 1671, the year before Drury Lane theatre was burnt down, the King granted the Duke of Bedford a licence for the market, so that it at last became legitimate; and a few years later twenty-three salesmen were registered there, licensed to sell flowers, fruit and vegetables on every day of the week except Sundays and Christmas Day. They also had permission to build cellars and shops all along the outside of the garden wall of Bedford House, but there were to be no chimneys, and the shops were to have uniform fronts and frontages one foot lower than the Bedford garden and not more than eight feet wide; the market people were 'to sit in order betwen the rails and the garden wall, from one to the other therof', thereby keeping well away from the centre of the square, which was a fashionable and pleasant promenade.

Much of the market produce was relatively new to England. Samuel Hartlib, writing in 1650, said that some old men, still living, remembered 'the first gardener who came into Surrey to plant cabbages, cauliflowers, and to sow turnips, carrots and peas, all of which at that time were great wonders, we having few or none in England but what came from Holland and Flanders'.

The dissolution of the monasteries a century or more earlier had had an unforeseen effect on English agriculture and horticulture, for the monks had been skilful farmers and gardeners. They had been able to exchange knowledge with visiting monks from Europe, who had access in their libraries to the agricultural knowledge of the classical writers. For a time this learning was almost lost, and not only did the cultivation of the fields become less efficient, but the kitchen gardens, with their herbs, fruit, vegetables and salads, began to disappear.

So barren did they become that, in Tudor times, such ordinary things as lettuces, cabbages and onions were being imported from Holland, because none were being grown here. But gradually, as the country entered a period of relative security and prosperity, seeds were brought from Holland, and people began once more to grow cabbages and onions, carrots and parsnips, turnips and cauliflowers. The market gardens of Fulham were laid out, to supply the citizens of London, and it was from here that much of the Covent Garden supplies now arrived.

Melons, pumpkins, radishes and 'all kinds of salad herbs' became popular again, and travellers brought back many more new plants from America and the Canaries, the Low Countries and the Mediterranean. The potato arrived, as well as apricot, almond, peach, fig, orange and lemon trees. As the art of grafting became more clearly understood, many improved strains of our own apple, pear, cherry, walnut and filbert trees were developed. Strawberries, raspberries and gooseberries were grown, and an astonishing number of herbs, which were used as much in the making of medicines and cosmetics as for cooking.

Along with the newly introduced vegetables came many new flowers to add to the English roses, daffodils, pansies and gillyflowers – Dutch tulips, nasturtiums, love-in-the-mist, honesty, larkspur, Christmas roses and passion-flowers, as well as the tulip-tree, syringa and red maple, while a few years later, Queen Henrietta Maria introduced the jasmine plant to England.

For many years the Stocks market in the City, held where the Mansion House now stands, was Covent Garden's nearest rival, but in the 1670s there was a much nearer threat, from the ill-fated Hungerford family, whose magnificent London mansion was close at hand, where Charing Cross station now stands.

A century or more earlier, Dame Agnes Hungerford had been attainted for the murder of her husband and hanged at Tyburn. He was the father of Sir Edward Hungerford, who lived through three marriages, treating each of his successive wives with shocking cruelty, and was himself executed at the same time as Thomas Cromwell, in 1540. His descendant, the next Edward Hungerford, created a Knight of the Bath at the coronation of Charles II, was a notorious spendthrift. He is said to have paid £500 for a wig to wear at a ball, and to have sold twenty-eight of the manors of his vast estates to settle his gambling debts. In 1669 his mansion in the Strand was nearly destroyed by fire, and he pulled down what was left of it and obtained permission to build a large market on the site, but the venture failed and Sir Edward, having squandered his entire fortune, died 'a poor Knight of Windsor' in 1711, at the age, it is said, of 115.

Amongst the aristocratic residents of Covent Garden during the Restoration years were Lord Brownlow, the Duke of Richmond, the Earl of Oxford, the Marquis of Windsor, the Earl of Sussex and the Earl of Peterborough, as well as the Bishop of Durham, of whom it was said that all the foundlings of Covent Garden were laid at his door, which is an unfortunately ambiguous statement. What happened to them no one knows, but they were at least christened, for a number of Peter, Paul and Mary Piazzas appeared in the register of St Paul's.

That strange character Sir Kenelm Digby came to live in the beautiful house in the north-west corner of the piazza – Number 43 King Street – until his death in 1665. He was the son of Sir Everard Digby who, when Kenelm was two years old, had been hanged for his part in the Gunpowder Plot. He had been born a Catholic but was sent to a Protestant tutor when he was a child, and then spent a year or two at Oxford. When he was twenty-two, he made a secret marriage with a childhood friend, 'that celebrated beautie and courtezane' Venetia Stanley, and after her early death, in 1633, he retired, broken-hearted, to Gresham College, where for two years he lived as a recluse, studying chemistry and the new discoveries of Harvey, Bacon and Galileo.

He seems to have been intrigued, but utterly bemused, by the developing scientific thought of the seventeenth century, and, for the most part, got everything wrong. 'He was the very Pliny of our age for lying,' wrote Stubbes.

He changed from Protestantism back to Catholicism, and then once more to Protestantism, to suit the mood of the hour, and published some fifteen books and treatises, none of which had any scientific merit; and he introduced to the world his 'powder of sympathy', a secret concoction which he claimed to have learned from a Carmelite who had travelled in the Far East. This was a 'powder of vitriol', to be used for the healing of wounds, but it did not have to be applied to the wound itself. Anything which the blood of the wound had touched, if immersed in the mystic powder, even though far distant from the sufferer, would effect an immediate cure – surely one of the oddest examples of sympathetic magic which, all too often, clouded these days of dawning enlightenment.

John Evelyn met him several times on his travels, during the days of the Commonwealth, and in 1650 they were both in Paris. 'Visited Sir Kenelm Digby,' wrote Evelyn, 'with whom I had much discourse on chemical matters ... He advised me to try and digest a little better, and gave me a water which he said was only rain-water of the autumnal equinox, exceedingly rectified, very volatile; it had a taste of strong vitriolic, and smelt like aqua-fortis. He intended it for a dissolvent of calx of gold; but the truth is, Sir Kenelm was an arrant mountebank.'

Back in London twenty years later, Evelyn mentions him again. He was at a dinner party at Goring House where Lord Stafford 'rose from table, in some disorder, because there were roses stuck about the fruit when the dessert was set on the table; such an antipathy, it seems, he had to them as once Lady Selenger also had, and to that degree that, as Sir Kenelm Digby tells us, laying but a rose upon her cheek when she was asleep, it raised a blister; but Sir Kenelm was a teller of strange things.' Yet he was one of the earliest members of the Royal Society.

A few years later, a pamphlet published in 1680 described another strange cure. Mother Trott was a good, kindly soul who sold apples, pears and oranges near the door of St Paul's, Covent Garden, and she was miserably unhappy because her only son, Jonathon, nineteen years of age, was grievously afflicted with glandular swellings in his neck which nearly choked him. The doctors said it was scrofula – the King's Evil – and they could do nothing for him. His only hope was to be 'touched' by the King, so Mrs Trott decided to undertake the long journey to Windsor with Jonathon the following day. However, that night 'she dreamt that she heard a voice that commanded her son to be touched by Mrs Fanshawe'. She was puzzled, for she had never heard of Mrs Fanshawe, and she was even more mystified when Jonathon told her 'he had heard a voice that night three times successively, telling him that one touch of Mrs Fanshawe would make him whole.'

They made enquiries and discovered that Mrs Fanshawe was in

1 Francis, 4th Earl of Bedford: the founder of Covent Garden

2 Inigo Jones: the builder of the piazza

3 Hollar's map of London showing Covent Garden

4 The arcades

5 William Wycherley, Restoration
dramatist, in 1668

6 Nell Gwynne in 1675

7 Act II Scene II of Settle's *Empress of Morocco* staged at the Duke's theatre, 1678

8 Self-portrait by Sir Peter Lely   9 Sir Godfrey Kneller

10 Joseph Addison in 1719

11 Sir Richard Steele in 1711

12 Memorial plaque to Charles Macklin   13 Macklin's house in Covent Garden

Sacred to the Memory
of CHARLES MACKLIN, Comedian:
This Tablet is Erected
(with the Aid of Public Patronage)
by his affectionate Widow ELIZABETH MACKLIN.
Obiit 11th July, 1797. Ætatis 107.

MACKLIN! the Father of the *modern Stage*
Renown'd alike for Talents and for Age.
Whose Years a Century and longer ran.
Who liv'd and dy'd *as may become a Man*.
This lasting Tribute to thy Worth receive.
'Tis all a grateful Public now can give.
Their loudest Plaudits now no more can move.
Yet hear! thy Widow's *still small Voice of Love*.

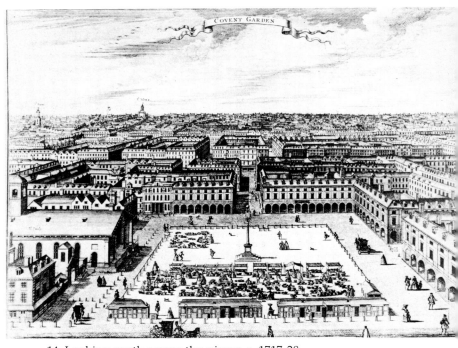

14 Looking north across the piazza *c.* 1717-28

15 Looking west in 1735

16 Joseph Van Aken's view of the market *c.* 1726-30

17 'Rich's Glory' by William Hogarth. John Rich opens his splendid new theatre, 7 December 1732

RICH'S GLORY *or his* Triumphant Entry *into* Covent-Garden.

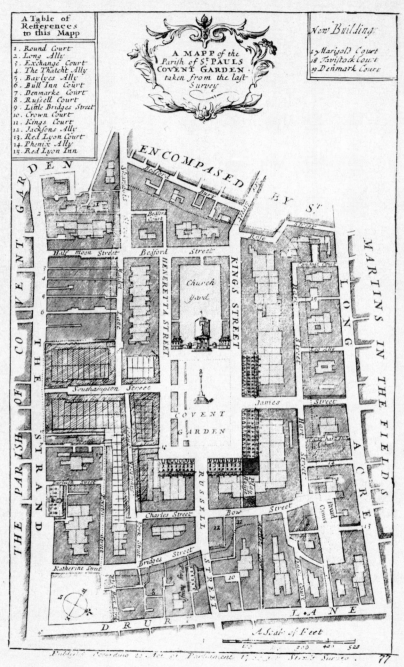

18 Map of Covent Garden in 1755, from *Stow's Survey*

fact Lucy Walter's daughter Mary, younger sister of the Duke of Monmouth, who a few weeks earlier had effected a wonderful cure on a young woman called Elizabeth Parcet.

So Jonathon took himself to Mrs Fanshawe's house near St James's, and 'as soon as ever Mrs Fanshawe appear'd, falling on his knees, he begged her to pardon him. Then, grasping her hands with all the violence and passion imaginable, kissed them a thousand times, and directed 'em ... to his neck, and his throat and all the other parts of his Body wherin he was afflicted, which she vouchsafed to stroke.' The youth then left her, confident that he would be speedily cured, and within three days he was 'perfectly and entirely cur'd, and Mrs Fanshawe by many of this person's Neighbours and acquaintances and most of all the apple-women of Covent Garden is to this day call'd Princess Fanshawe'.

The cure may well have been an example of faith healing, but the story was almost certainly circulated by Lucy Walter's relations in Covent Garden to confirm the fact that, despite the apparent impossibility, Mary Fanshawe was indeed the King's daughter and had thereby acquired a measure of the sacred healing properties still attributed to royalty.

All the Stuart monarchs touched for the King's Evil, and Charles II is said to have touched more than 93,000 people during his reign. The sufferer had to touch the royal person, and the monarch crossed the sores of the sick person with a silver coin, which he then gave him to hang round his neck until he was cured.

A few weeks after the Restoration, Pepys, being in Whitehall, stayed to see the King touch people for the King's Evil. 'But he did not come at all, it rayned so: and the poor people were forced to stand all morning in the rain in the garden. Afterwards he touched them in the Banqueting-house.'

The following April, again being in Whitehall, he says that 'I went to the Banqueting house, and there saw the King heal, the first time that ever I saw him do it; which he did with great gravity, and it seemed to me to be an ugly office and a simple one.'

William III would have nothing to do with the practice, dismissing it as 'popish nonsense', but Queen Anne revived it. 'Young Johnson,' wrote Boswell, 'had the misfortune to be much afflicted with scrofula, or King's Evil, which disfigured a countenance naturally well formed, and hurt his visual nerves so much, that he did not see at all with one of his eyes, though its appearance was little different from that of the other ... It has been said that he contracted this grievous malady from his nurse. His mother yielding to the superstitious notion, which it is wonderful to think, prevailed so long in this country, as to the virtue of the regal touch ... carried him to London, where he was actually touched by Queen Anne. Mrs Johnson indeed ... acted by the advice of the celebrated Sir John Floyer, then a physician in Lichfield.'

Johnson was only two and a half years old at the time, but he told Boswell he had a dim recollection of 'a lady in diamonds, and a long black hood'. The touch, however, 'was without any effect'; and with the accession of the Hanoverians, the practice was discontinued.

Sir Peter Lely had his studio in the piazza, the house being in the north-west corner, where later the Tavistock Hotel was to be built. He was born in Westphalia in 1618 but had arrived in London by the time he was twenty-three and remained until his death; and it was here that he painted his portraits of Frances Stuart, Anne Hyde, Duchess of York, Louise, Duchess of Portsmouth, and Barbara, Duchess of Cleveland, as well as Nell Gwynne; and in 1680 he was buried in St Paul's churchyard.

His successor, Sir Godfrey Kneller, also lived in the square, at a house on the site of the Floral Hall. He was born in Germany but in 1678 arrived in England as a student touring Europe. The Duke of Monmouth was the first to appreciate his work and recommended him to Charles II, who had soon appointed him Court Painter. He lived in the square for the next twenty-one years and was to be the painter to five sovereigns in succession. He painted the forty-two members of the Kit-Kat Club and many members of the Court and Society, including Nell Gwynne, who commissioned a portrait from him during the last year or two of her short life.

In an advertisement some years later, Kneller's house was described as having a front room 42 feet by 19 feet and 12 feet high, with a garden attached to the mansion 150 feet by 40 feet. His next-door neighbour was the irascible Dr Radcliffe, whose benificence to Oxford was the basis of the Radcliffe Library. Kneller ultimately moved to Great Queen Street, where he opened an academy for his fellow artists, and Sir James Thornhill moved into his Covent Garden house.

Kneller, too, was buried at St Paul's, when he died in 1723, but in listing the famous who were buried in this small spot, we must not forget the infamous. Claude Duval, the highwayman, was a

Frenchman who had come to England as a valet after the Restoration, but he soon took to the road, leading a gang of robbers who haunted the northern approaches of London, particularly Holloway, between Islington and Highgate.

The story goes that 'at the head of his troop, he stopped a lady's coach, in which there was a booty of £400: but he took only £100' and 'suffered the fair owner to ransom the rest by dancing a coranto with him on the Heath'. True or not, it was a tale to fire the imagination of those romantically minded young women who had not had first-hand experience of him, although the unfortunates who had met him must have found him infuriating. In 1669, when he was twenty-seven years old, Claude Duval was at last captured at Mother Maberley's tavern in Chandos Street, 'The-Hole-In-The-Wall'. He was brought to trial, and when he was hanged at Tyburn, the watching crowds were loud in their lamentations. His body was cut down and brought to the Tangier Tavern in St Giles for a 'lying-in-state', and then he was given a grand funeral at St Paul's, attended with flambeaux and followed by a long train of mourners, 'to the great grief of the women'. He is said to have been buried under the central aisle of the church, with an epitaph which ran:

Here lies Duval. Reader, if male thou art
Look to thy purse, if female, to thy heart.

But there is no trace of that epitaph today, and it is said that his body was long ago taken away to some unknown spot for a fresh burial.

In 1679, while Kneller was painting his masterpieces in his house in the piazza, Dryden was living in Rose Street, off Long Acre, and on a dark night of December, as he was on his way home, he was attacked by a gang of masked bullies. A reward of £50 was offered for the discovery of his assailants and lodged at Child's Bank in the Strand, but no one ever came forward to claim it. Yet it became almost certain that the attack had been at the instigation of the Earl of Rochester, encouraged by Louise, Duchess of Portsmouth. The Earl had at one time been friendly with Lord Mulgrave, who was also a friend of Dryden's. The Earl and Lord Mulgrave quarrelled, and shortly afterwards a satire was circulated, reputed to have been written by Mulgrave, which attacked not only Rochester but the Duchesses of Cleveland and Portsmouth and also the King. And Dryden was thought, quite wrongly, to have helped Musgrave in the writing of it.

It was during these early years of the Restoration that the Hummums, a Turkish bath establishment, was opened on the south-west corner of Russell Street, facing the market and part of the Little Piazza. For a few years it was very popular amongst the residents, but then it fell on evil times and became dirty and neglected and haunted by prostitutes.

Far more successful were the new coffee-houses. Coffee had become popular throughout the East towards the end of the previous century, and during the following years samples were brought to Europe, where it soon became a fashionable drink. The first coffee-houses were opened in Constantinople and Venice. In 1652 Bowman opened a coffee-house in St Michael's, Cornhill, and after that they grew extremely popular, to the temporary dismay of the brewers and vintners. Coffee-houses became more than places for drinking coffee, for they met a long-felt need as meeting-places for merchants to exchange news and business, and were also places for the gathering of the two main political groups, some becoming the forerunners of the eighteenth-century clubs. The government made several attempts to suppress the coffee-houses, complaining that they were the breeding grounds of sedition. Beer, they said, was preferable to coffee, because coffee was a stimulant which kept people awake and made them more inclined to rebellion, while somnolent beer kept them loyal; and in the years to come, at election times, the Tories always drank beer and jeered at the Whigs and their coffee, which they described as a 'syrop of soot and old shoes'.

Chocolate also became fashionable as a drink about this time, having been brought by Cortez from Mexico to Spain. According to one recipe, its preparation was no light task. The cocoa nibs were lightly crushed and boiled for several hours, with white sugar, cinnamon, Mexican peppers, cloves, almonds, orange-flower water and vanilla straws, and then 'enriched with milk and beaten eggs'.

Tea was first brought to Europe by merchants of the Dutch East India Company, as a gift to the royal family of Orange. They liked it, and tea-drinking became popular amongst the Dutch aristocracy. When the Dutch Company introduced it to England, it became just as fashionable amongst those who could afford to buy it, but the first consignments cost anything up to £10 a pound, so it was far beyond the reach of most people.

However, the British East India Company, which had been

granted its charter in 1600, was very soon bringing in supplies of tea at more reasonable prices, and in 1637 Thomas Garraway announced from his coffee-house in Exchange Alley that he had acquired supplies of tea, the best quality of which he could sell at 50 shillings a pound, the lowest at as little as 16 shillings.

This was still too expensive for most people, but for the prosperous and fashionable it was welcomed. Tea was considered to have medicinal qualities, and many doctors recommended it, particularly the Dutch doctor Cornelius Bontekoe, who advised the taking of at least ten cups every day. On the other hand, some years later Dr John Soames, the doctor in attendance at the Hampstead spa, declared that tea was reducing the stature of the nation, and if people continued to drink it, it would cause 'the next generation to be more like pygmies than men and women'. He apparently had a grudge against tea, although he was obviously a smoker. 'They that take tobacco may do it here with all the safety in the World,' he said, 'but let them have a regard not to offend the company, especially the ladies, who cannot well relish the smoke with their waters.'

Tea, chocolate and sherbert were served in the coffee-houses, as well as coffee, all of it drawn from large barrels.

In 1660 Pepys recorded that, 'I did send for a cup of tea, a China drink of which I never had drunk before,' and he soon became a regular tea-drinker.

Women were not allowed inside the coffee-houses, so took to tea-drinking in their own homes, keeping the precious leaves locked up in beautifully decorated tea-caddies. Some of the early brews must have been very strange, though, for the mystique of tea-making had not yet had time to develop. A Jesuit returning from China said that, 'the hot water should not stay upon the tea leaves any longer than you can say the Miserere Psalm very leisurely', but in 1668, when the Duchess of Monmouth sent some tea to friends in Scotland, as a gift, they boiled the leaves, threw away the liquid and tried to eat what was left as a vegetable.

In Covent Garden, the most popular coffee-houses were around Russell Street, which, crossing Bow Street, was the direct way from the piazza to the Theatre Royal in Drury Lane. In its heyday, during the last few decades of the seventeenth century, Will's was the first to become famous. It stood at the northern corner of Russell Street and Bow Street and had formerly been a tavern called the 'Red Cow'. The ground floor was a haberdasher's shop, but on the first floor Will

Urwin opened his coffee-shop. Dryden was his most distinguished customer, one of the few men of letters who was accepted during his lifetime as the greatest writer of his day, and it was Dryden who made Will Urwin's fortune. Will's customers were seated for the most part in groups at small tables, but Dryden held the place of honour, by the fire in winter, and in a corner of the balcony overlooking the street in summer. 'Nowhere was the smoking more constant than at Will's,' wrote Macaulay. 'That celebrated house, situated between Covent Garden and Bow Street, was sacred to polite letters. There the talk was about poetical justice and the unities of time and place … One group debated whether "Paradise Lost" ought not to have been in rhyme. To another an envious poetaster demonstrated that "Venice Preserved" ought to have been hooted from the stage … The great press was to get near the chair where John Dryden sat. To bow to the Laureate and to hear his opinion of Racine's last tragedy, or of Bossu's treatise on Epic poetry, was thought a privilege. A pinch from his snuff-box was an honour sufficient to turn the head of a young enthusiast.'

Pepys, walking one winter's night through Covent Garden to fetch home his wife, said: 'I stopped at the great Coffee-house there, where I never was before; where Dryden the poet (I knew him at Cambridge), and all the wits of the town … And had I had time then, or could at other times, it will be good coming thither, for there, I perceive, is very witty and pleasant discourse … '

So distinguished did the company of listeners become, when Dryden held court, that although Will's did not have the rules and subscription of the clubs which were soon to come into existence, it was really one of the first literary clubs in London, and few would have presumed to visit it without a proper introduction.

Pope, who was not born until 1688, had so deep an admiration for the great Dryden that he persuaded some friends to take him to Will's, to gaze upon the great man. Dryden died in 1700, so Pope cannot have been more than twelve at the time, but he never forgot that visit.

This was the year that Tom's Coffee House was established by Captain Thomas West close by, and very soon it became as famous as Will's for its distinguished customers. Here again, the coffee-house occupied the upper part of the house, the ground floor being let to T. Lewis, a bookseller and publisher, who first brought out Pope's *Essay on Criticism*.

'After the play,' wrote Macky, in his *Journey Through England,* 'the best company usually go to Tom's and Will's Coffee Houses, near adjoining, where there is playing at Picket, and the best conversation till midnight ... ' In those early days, the coffee-house was 'crowded with noblemen in their stars and garters, drinking their tea and coffee, exposed to the people, while at the upper windows, with their balconies, were to be seen such frequenters as were not engaged in reading the news-sheets or in playing cards'.

In 1722 Captain West, racked with pain through gout, committed suicide by throwing himself from one of the bedroom windows, but the coffee-house passed into other hands and remained as popular throughout the whole of the eighteenth century, during which many more illustrious names were to be associated with it.

During the early years of the reign of George III a club was formed here, which eventually was called the Literary Club and had seven hundred members, including David Garrick, Samuel Foote, Sir John Fielding, Lord Clive, Oliver Goldsmith and Dr Johnson.

Tom's continued until 1814, when the place was taken over by a numismatist called Till, and the club ceased to exist. Till wrote: 'The house in which I reside was the famous Tom's Coffee House, memorable in the reign of Queen Anne, and for more than half a century afterwards: the room in which I conduct my business as a coin dealer, is that which, in 1764, by a guinea subscription among nearly seven hundred of the nobility, foreign ministers, gentry and geniuses of the age – was made the card-room and place of meeting, of many of the now illustrious dead, and remained so till 1768, when a voluntary subscription among its members induced Mr Haines, the then proprietor (and the father of the present occupier of the house), to take in the next room westwards, as a coffee-room; and the whole floor, en suite, was constructed into card and conversation rooms.'

After Till's death the place continued as a numismatist's for some years, but in 1865 the building was demolished and a bank built on the site.

Joseph Addison and Sir Richard Steele are the next two great literary figures associated with Covent Garden. They were both born in 1672 and met at school at Charterhouse. Both began writing while still in their teens, and both grew up to be Whigs.

Addison's earliest poems were in Latin but his first English poem, written when he was only twenty-one and still at Oxford was *To Mr Dryden.* Dryden greatly appreciated the compliment and was impressed with the young poet. They met and Dryden introduced him to many of the important Whig leaders of the day and also to Jacob Tonson, the bookseller and publisher of the Strand, who had already published much of Dryden's work and was to become the publisher of both Addison and Pope.

After four years abroad, making the Grand Tour, Addison was elected a member of the Kit-Kat Club, the Whig club which was founded in 1700. Its origins are obscure, and it may well have begun as a weekly dinner party given by Tonson himself for his distinguished authors. At its foundation there were thirty-nine members, all men of letters and the arts, wits, noblemen and men of considerable substance, united by a common concern to secure the Protestant succession and put an end to the last hopes of the Stuarts.

From the beginning, Jacob Tonson was the secretary and they met at the Cat and Fiddle in Shoe Lane, the shop of a pastry cook named Christopher Kat, who made a particularly good mutton pie which he dubbed a Kit-Kat. Among the members were six dukes, including the Duke of Marlborough, as well as Lord Halifax, Sir Robert Walpole, the Earl of Dorset, Congreve, Sir Samuel Garth, Vanbrugh, Addison, Steele and Godfrey Kneller, and it was Kneller who, as we have seen, painted all thirty-nine members for Tonson, which now hang in the National Portrait Gallery. Alexander Pope, being a Roman Catholic, was not a member. The club lasted until around 1727, when George II came to the throne and the Hanoverian succession seemed secure.

Richard Steele had been nominated to Charterhouse by the Duke of Ormonde, who had known Covent Garden so well, for Steele's father had died when Richard was a child and the family was left by no means well off. After leaving Oxford, Steele came to London, where he was publishing poetry while still in his early twenties. He joined the literary circle at Will's Coffee House, and in 1701 his first play was produced, two more following within the next three or four years. They were not great plays, but they marked a change in the style of dramatic entertainment in England, for they were gentle, romantic comedies and a reaction from the indecencies of Wycherley and Congreve, which Jeremy Collier had so severely condemned. These first three plays and a fourth, written some years later, are all basically moral and even sentimental.

In 1707 Steele was appointed editor of the *London Gazette*, the City's official news sheet, and one of many which came into existence at this time, before Parliamentary verbatim reporting was possible, but which tried, nevertheless, to report contemporary home and foreign news. Two years later he launched the *Tatler*, a very different kind of publication, which might be called the first magazine. Its purpose was to describe and criticize society in London, although at first he did include a certain amount of news too. In the opening number, a double-column folio sheet, which appeared on 12 April 1709, he wrote that the paper was 'for the use of political persons, who are so public-spirited as to neglect their own affairs to look into transactions of state' and that 'such worthy and well-affected members of the commonwealth may be instructed, after their reading, what to THINK.'

The subjects for the first articles were gathered from the 'various resorts of the town'. 'Thus,' wrote Steele, 'all accounts of gallantry, pleasure and entertainment are under the article of White's Chocolate House; Poetry under that of Will's Coffee House; learning under the title of the Grecian; Foreign and Domestick News from St James's Coffee House.' But the foreign news was soon dropped and the paper became concerned purely with social matters, for Steele was essentially bent on reforming society.

Addison had been absorbed in both writing and politics after his return from his European tour, but with the fall of the Whig government in 1710, and the consequent loss of his appointment as an Under-Secretary of State, he was free to help Steele with his new venture.

The *Tatler* was published at the price of a penny, on Tuesdays, Thursdays and Saturdays, these being the days when the post left London for the country, and each number contained three or four articles on such diverse subjects as dramatic criticism, a gentle satire on the fopperies of dress and conversation, a serious discourse on the evils of gaming and duelling, and the tragedy of loveless marriages.

Steele wrote, for example: 'It is with great indignation that I see such crowds of the female world lost to human society, and condemned to a laziness which makes life pass away with less relish than in the hardest labour ... Those who are in the quality of gentlewomen should propose to themselves some suitable method of passing away their time. This would furnish them with reflections and sentiments proper for the companions of reasonable men, and prevent the unnatural marriages which happen every day between the most accomplish'd women and the veriest oafs, the worthiest men and the most insignificant females. Were the general run of women's education of another kind than it is at present, we should want one another for more reasons than we do as the world now goes.'

Yet it was not for another half a century that the Bluestockings began to hold their gatherings at Mrs Elizabeth Montagu's house in Mayfair.

Addison in the *Tatler* was amusing about quack doctors, who were still doing good business throughout the country. 'There are some who have gained themselves great reputation for physic by their birth, as in "seventh son of a seventh son" ... I remember when our whole island was shaken with an earthquake some years ago, there was an impudent mountebank who sold pills, which (as he told the country people) were very good against an earthquake ... '

The *Tatler* lasted until 2 January 1711, and of the 271 numbers published during this time Addison contributed more than sixty articles, while Steele wrote 188 himself and 25 in collaboration with Addison.

The two friends now produced their daily sheet the *Spectator*, which also cost a penny until the Stamp Act, when the price had to be raised to 2d. The first issue was on 1 March 1711, and it ran until December 1712, during which time Steele wrote 236 and Addison 274 of the 555 numbers.

The *Spectator* was a more solid literary paper, written in a rather more serious vein than the *Tatler*, and they followed it with the short-lived *Guardian*, which ran from March to October 1713, the year that Addison's play *Cato* was produced at Drury Lane.

The articles in the *Guardian* were written in much the same vein as before, Addison writing, for example, on Naked Bosoms: 'There are many little enormities in the world, which our preachers would be very glad to see removed, but at the same time dare not meddle with, for fear of betraying the dignity of the pulpit ... For this reason, I look upon myself to be of great use to these good men; while they are employed in extirpating mortal sins and crimes of a higher nature, I should be glad to rally the whole world out of indecencies and venial transgression ... This much I thought fit to premise before I resume the subject which I have already handled, I mean the naked bosoms of our British ladies. I hope they will not take it ill of me, if I still beg that they will be covered ... '

After the death of Dryden, Will's was never the same. It remained popular for a time, but the standard of discourse was not so high. By the time he was seventeen, Alexander Pope, already a poet of distinction, was visiting Will's on his own account, but Jonathon Swift, a distant relative of Dryden, although thirty years younger, wrote sourly of the company he found there in later years. The worst conversation he ever heard in his life, he said 'was at Will's Coffee-house, where the wits (as they were called) used formally to assemble; that is to say, five or six men, who had writ plays or at least prologues, or had a share in a miscellany, came thither, and entertained one another with their trifling composures, in so important an air, as if they had been the noblest efforts of human nature, or that the fate of kingdoms depended on them.'

It was for only about ten years that Will's maintained its prestige, and then Will Urwin retired, the place becoming a famous ham and beef shop.

Button's Coffee House, opening in 1712 on the opposite side of Russell Street, now became popular. Daniel Button had been a servant of the widowed Countess of Warwick, with whom Addison was in love and whom he was to marry a few years later, and it was he who set up Button.

With the production of Addison's *Cato*, the coffee-house achieved its literary reputation. 'Covent Garden is the Heart of the Town,' said Steele, and Button's became the centre of the literary world. Here Addison established his lion's head, which was designed by Christopher Wren, by this time in his eighties. In July 1713 Addison wrote in the *Guardian*: 'It is my intention to erect a lion's head, in imitation of those I have described in Venice, through which all the private commonwealth is said to pass. This head is to open a most wide and voracious mouth, which shall take in such letters and papers as are conveyed to me by my correspondents ... There will be under it a box, of which the key will be in my own custody, to receive such papers as are dropped into it. Whatever the lion swallows I shall digest for the use of the public.' And a fortnight later he was writing: ' ... the lion's head is now erected at Button's Coffee-house, in Russell Street, Covent Garden, where it opens its mouth at all hours for the reception of such intelligence as shall be thrown into it. It is reckoned an excellent piece of workmanship, and was designed by a great hand in imitation of the antique Egyptian lion, the face of it being compounded out of that of a lion and a wizard. The features are strong and well-furrowed. The whiskers are admired by all that have seen them. It is planted on the western side of the coffee house, holding its paws under the chin, upon a box, which contains everything that he swallows. He is, indeed, a proper emblem of knowledge and action, being all head and paws.'

Pope used to visit Button's when it first opened. 'Addison usually studied all the morning,' he wrote, 'then met his party at Button's, dined there, and stayed five or six hours, and sometimes far into the night. I was of the company for about a year, but found it too much for me; it hurt my health, and so I quitted it.'

But Pope was far from popular at Button's, for he had a bitter, often jealous tongue, and Colley Cibber once wrote to him: 'When you used to pass your hours at Button's, you were even then remarkable for your satirical itch of provocation, scarce was there a gentleman of any pretentions to wit whom your unguarded temper had not fallen upon in some biting epigram; among whom you once caught a pastoral Tartar, whose resentment, that your punishment might be proportional to the smart of your poetry, had stuck up a birchen rod in the room, to be ready whenever you might come within reach of it; and at this rate you writ and rallied and writ on till you rhymed yourself quite out of the coffee house.'

In 1716 Addison at last married the Countess of Warwick and lived with her at Holland House. The marriage was said to have been unhappy, but that may well have been quite untrue, and a result of Pope's spiteful comment that Addison had 'married discord' and that it was to Button's that he used to retreat 'whenever he suffered any vexation from the Countess'.

But it sounds like the plight of poor Wycherley, some years earlier, who, with his first wife, the Countess of Drogheda, lodged by the Cock tavern in Bow Street, for the Countess, 'though a splendid wife, was not formed to make a man happy'. In fact, she was so jealous of him that whenever he slipped into the Cock for a quiet drink, 'he was obliged to leave the windows open that his lady might see there was no woman in the company.' However, his troubles came to an end in due course, for the Countess 'made him some amends by dying in reasonable time.'

Early in 1714 Steele was elected to Parliament, but a few weeks later, because two pamphlets he had published, *The Crisis* and *The Englishman*, were regarded as seditious, he was expelled. However, with the death of Queen Anne later in the year, the accession of George I and the return to power of the Whigs, he was again in Parliament, being knighted the following year, while Addison was made Chief Secretary for Ireland.

Addison was appointed a Secretary of State in 1717, but he was already a sick man, and less than a year later he had to resign office, spending most of his time in retirement at Holland House.

Steele's turn of good fortune did not last. In 1718 he lost a great deal of money in an unsound business speculation, but far worse than this was the death of his second wife, his 'dear Prue', a shock from which he never fully recovered. Early in the following year he quarrelled with Addison over the policies of the Peerage Bill. It proved the end of the long friendship which had meant so much to them both, for before it could be mended Addison died, at Holland House, in 1719.

Steele launched another short-lived periodical, *The Theatre*, and wrote one or two more pamphlets and plays, but by this time he was so heavily in debt that he had to leave London. He stayed for a time with his friend Bishop Hoadly at Hereford, and then moved on to a property of Prue's in Carmarthen, where, in 1729, he died of a stroke, 'though retaining his cheerful sweetness of temper to the last ... '.

Button's business dwindled sadly after this, many of his customers drifting away to the Bedford Coffee House, in the north-east corner of the piazza, or the Shakespeare tavern, which was next to the Piazza Coffee House; and by the time he died, in 1731, he was receiving parish relief from St Paul's. He was buried in St Paul's graveyard, and on his tombstone was carved the inscription:

Odds fish, and fiery coals,
Are graves become Button-holes!

His coffee-house soon became a private residence again, but the Lion's Head was saved and was ultimately bought by the Russell family and moved to Woburn Abbey.

During the last days of Button's, one of its visitors was Jemmy Maclaine, the 'Gentleman Highwayman'. He was much taken with Button's daughter, who acted as barmaid. Another visitor, Mr Donaldson, recognized Jemmy and told Button to warn his daughter, but the silly girl, captivated by Jemmy's charm, warned Jemmy instead. The next time he saw Donaldson in Button's, he called him out. 'Mr Donaldson, I wish to speak to you in a private room,' he said. Donaldson, being unarmed, refused, saying he knew of nothing that could not be said between them in public. 'Very well. We shall meet again,' replied Jemmy. A few days later, as Donaldson was walking in Richmond Park, he saw Jemmy riding towards him and prepared for a fight, but at the last minute Jemmy saw a carriage approaching and, deciding that the prospect of more plunder was a better proposition than punishing Donaldson, changed his mind and gave chase to it, giving Donaldson the chance to make his escape.

Jemmy had a long run for his money. In 1749 he robbed and slightly wounded Horace Walpole, walking in Hyde Park, on his way back from Holland House, but he was caught in the end, and on the first Sunday after his condemnation, three thousand people went to visit him in his cell at Newgate prison; he is said to have fainted twice with the heat and pressure of the admirers who crowded round him for his last appearance, before his execution at Tyburn on 3 October 1750.

5

Gin and Justices

London was growing quickly, and Inigo Jones had begun an architectural fashion which was to spread throughout the city. In 1665 John Evelyn, describing a visit to the Earl of Southampton, wrote: 'dined at my Lord Treasurer, the Earl of Southampton, in Bloomsbury, where he was building a noble square, or piazza, a little town; his own house stands too low, some noble rooms, a pretty cedar chapel, a naked garden to the north, but good air.' This was Southampton Square, which soon became as fashionable as Covent Garden, and here, in 1704, the Russell family moved from Covent Garden to the Earl of Southampton's house, calling it Bedford House, while the square became known as Bloomsbury Square.

Building was also going on to the west of Covent Garden. Leicester Fields became Leicester Square. Soho Square, at first called King's Square, where the Duke of Monmouth had a house, was built soon afterwards, with its surrounding streets.

Charles II had granted Lord Clarendon a site amongst the fields to the north of Piccadilly, where he built his magnificent Clarendon House, which was completed in 1667, but his star was fast sinking, and by the end of that year he had to escape secretly to France, to avoid arrest. Six years later, the house on which he had lavished such loving care was demolished. 'They design a new town as it were, and a most magnificent piazza,' wrote Evelyn. 'I was astonished at the demolition, no less than at the little army of labourers and artificers levelling the ground, laying foundations and contriving great buildings ... '

However, the syndicate planning the square ran into money troubles, and it was never built. On the south side of Piccadilly, St James's Square was laid out, and a few years later Bond Street and Albemarle Street were built on the site of Clarendon House, while more mansions went up in Piccadilly, including Burlington House and Berkeley House, and within the next decade the Mayfair squares were being developed.

In Covent Garden, the deserted Bedford House was demolished, and in its place Tavistock Street and Southampton Street were built and Bedford Street extended.

In 1689 Strype had written: 'The south side of Covent Garden Square lieth open to Bedford House, where there is a small grotto of trees, most pleasant in the summer season; and on this side is kept a market for fruits, herbs, roots and flowers ... which is grown to a considerable account, and well served with choice goods, which make it much resorted to.'

It was not yet as large as the Stocks market in the City, and until the demolition of Bedford House it was still restricted to the line of stalls and sheds on the south side. Now, however, the change began. To serve the increasing number of people living in the surrounding streets, the market gradually spread into the square, and the salesmen – the small hucksters and retail dealers – began to build sleeping-accommodation over their stalls. The residents protested to the Russells, but all in vain. The market did not change. On the contrary, it continued to spread. The central part of the square was still protected with its wooden railings for some years, and the column remained until 1790, but now old women sat on its steps, selling bowls of milk and porridge. Many of the wealthy residents began to move away to the even grander houses of the new streets and squares farther west, and their houses in the piazza were usually let out as smaller apartments, some of them very soon becoming gambling houses or brothels. But the process was gradual. For example, after the death of Sir Kenelm Digby, his house was occupied by Admiral Russell, Earl of Orford for a time. Then Lord Archer moved there, until his death in 1768, and James West for the next four years, after which it became Evans' supper-rooms and hotel.

The Hummums took on a new lease of life, for in 1701 it was announced that 'the Hummums in Covent Garden having for several years past been neglected and abused by those persons that had the care and management of them, whereby several persons of quality have been disgusted, and have left off coming thither to sweat and bathe as formerly: This is to give notice that the said Hummums are now in possession of others, who have refitted the same and rectified all those neglects and abuses that were formerly done there, where persons may bathe in the cleanliest, and be cupped after the newest manner. There is likewise provided good lodging for any persons who shall desire to lodge there all night, where who pleases may see the same. The prices, as was always, for sweating and bathing, is 5/6, for two in one room 8/-: but who lodges there all night 10/-.'

In 1710 Martin Powell established his puppet show, which he had brought from Bath, under the Little Piazza, and it proved immensely popular. 'What man or child that lives within the verge of Covent Garden, or what beau, belle or visitant of Bath, knows not Mr Powell?' asked Burnet.

He showed the stories of Robin Hood and Little John, Friar Bacon and Friar Bungay, a mock opera, *Venus and Adonis*, or *The Triumph of Love*, and well-tried favourites such as Mother Goose.

Here is one of Powell's advertisements. 'At Punch's Theatre, in the Little Piazza, this present Friday, being the 2nd, and tomorrow, the 3rd of May, will be presented an opera, called the "State of Innocence, or the Fall of Man", with variety of scenes and machines, particularly the scene of Paradise in its primitive state, with birds, beasts, and all its ancient inhabitants, the subtlety of the serpent in betraying Adam and Eve, etc., with variety of diverting interludes, too many to be inserted here. No person to be admitted in masks or riding hoods (commonly used at the other theatres for the purpose of licentious intrigue), nor any money to be returned after the curtain is up. Boxes 2/s; pit 1s. Beginning exactly at seven o'clock.'

In 1704 Sir John Vanbrugh raised £3,000 from thirty subscribers, each with a £100 share, to build a small opera house in the Haymarket, which he designed himself. The theatre opened the following year with an Italian opera, *The Triumph of Love*, but it was a dismal failure and was withdrawn, after only three performances, to a wretchedly small audience. Sir John and his principal associate, Congreve, withdrew from the venture as soon as they could, but nevertheless the little theatre continued to present opera, and when George I succeeded, he patronized it often and the house was called the King's Theatre. Yet opera was not accepted by most English people for a long time to come. 'The Italian opera stole into England at the beginning of the eighteenth century,' wrote Colley Cibber, 'but in as rude a disguise as possible, in a lame, hobbling translation, with metre out of measure in its original notes, sung by our own unskilful voices, with graces misapplied to almost every sentiment and action,' while thirty years later Horace Walpole, writing about Vaneschi's opera *Fetonte*, said: 'They sing to jigs, and dance to church music. "Phaeton" is run away with by horses that go a foot's pace, like the Electress's coach, with such long traces, that the postilion was in one street and the coachman in another. Then comes "Jupiter" with a farthing candle, to light a squib and a half; and that they call fireworks. "Reginello", the first man, is so old and so tall, that he seems to have been growing ever since the invention of operas. The first woman has had her mouth let out to show a fine set of teeth, but it lets out too much bad voice at the same time ... ' *

Rich continued to pay his way at Drury Lane by putting on, to the indignation of the true actors in his company, any form of entertainment which he thought might bring in money, but it was through his meanness over money matters that he was at last ousted. Colley Cibber, Doggett and Wilks formed a joint management at Drury Lane, while Rich retreated to the Lincoln's Inn theatre, which he set about rebuilding.

The grand old actor Betterton was failing in health, and in 1710 he died, but his pupil Barton Booth now rose to fame at Drury Lane, his first great triumph coming when he played the name part in Addison's play *Cato*; and before long he had replaced Doggett as one of the three actor-managers. But it was while Doggett was still at the Lane that he inaugurated the Doggett Coat and Badge race for Thames lightermen, to celebrate the accession of George I and the Hanoverians. In the early days it was run every year on 1 August by young watermen who had just completed their apprenticeship, on the 4½-mile stretch of the river between London Bridge and Chelsea, and the prize, a doublet, breeches and hose, with a silver badge, was presented at the Fishmongers' Hall. The race fell into abeyance for a time but within recent years has been revived.

Successful as Barton Booth undoubtedly was at the Lane, the art of acting was developing very slowly. Actors, in their periwigs and full-skirted coats, still used the old, formalized gestures and declaimed their speeches from the apron, and it was perhaps small wonder that Rich prospered at Lincoln's Inn Fields, with his less formal and more varied entertainments.

* The theatre was burnt to the ground in 1789, said to have been arson on the part of the leader of the orchestra, who owed the manager a grudge. It was rebuilt and, with the accession of Queen Victoria, was known as 'Her Majesty's'.

During these years, the population of London, and with it the district of Covent Garden, was still growing steadily, and unemployment was rife. The destitution in London was appalling, and Gregory King estimated that by the early years of the eighteenth century nearly one in four of the population was out of work, while for thousands more wages were so low that they were barely above subsistence level; their only hope of survival was from poor relief, administered by the justices, who were notoriously corrupt and inefficient. The result was a widespread increase of theft and crimes of violence, intensified by the easy availability of cheap gin, which had been introduced to England by King William of Orange and his Dutch friends. At first, gin was imported, but very soon it was being distilled from English corn, and its manufacture was encouraged because, according to Defoe, it consumed such large quantities of grain that the farmers and large landowners reaped handsome profits. After import duties were imposed on French wine and brandy, during the long quarrel with France, gin was distilled in England in such quantities that it was cheaper than beer, and during the 1730s and 1740s there were some seven thousand gin shops in London alone, causing so many deaths that for a few years the death rate was higher than the birth rate.

'The retailers of this poisonous compound,' said Smollett, 'set up painted boards in public inviting people to be drunk for the small expense of one penny, and assuring them they might be dead drunk for twopence and have straw for nothing.

'As his guests get intoxicated they are laid together promiscuously, men, women and children, till they recover their senses, when they proceed to get drunk again, or having spent all they had, go out to find wherewithal to return to the same dreadful pursuit, and how they acquire more money the sessions paper too often acquaints us.'

It was not until the Gin Act of 1751, when a new duty was imposed and retailers had to be licensed, that matters began to improve a little, but with no proper means of enforcement, there were plenty of ways of evading the new law. The smuggling business flourished and crime grew more violent, while an increasing number of women took to prostitution.

At the beginning of Georgian times, justice in England was administered as it had been since medieval times, by unpaid Justices of the Peace. These men were chosen from the local gentry, by the Lord Lieutenant of the county, to govern their district for the

Crown, and their duties included levying the county rate, maintaining roads and bridges, the · licensing of taverns, the administration of the Poor Law and the supervision of houses of correction, prisons and workhouses. All this they administered either at the quarter and petty session or from their own homes.

Constables, whose task it was to help the magistrates and maintain law and order, were also unpaid citizens, who took yearly office in rotation.

Justices of the Peace were allowed certain fees for expenses, but it was not until the end of the century that stipendiary magistrates, with regular incomes, were instituted. In the country districts, men of integrity could usually be found to fulfil the duties required of them, but in the large towns, and particularly in London, where the duties became yearly more exacting, there was a growing tendency to corruption.

Punishments for wrong-doing were severe. As late as 1769 there were 160 offences listed for which the penalty was death by hanging, including smuggling, highway robbery and cattle-thieving. Magistrates were often merciful and found loopholes in the law, but during the early years of the century an average of twenty people were hanged each year in London alone, some for the theft of only a few shillings, and public hangings were often treated as free entertainment.

As for debtors, they were committed to prison and stayed there until the money was paid or they died from hunger or gaol fever. Worse still, they were committed to prison before trial and often had to wait for months before their cases were heard. The prisons were terrible places, without light, sanitation, ventilation or heat. Prisoners awaiting trial were expected to provide their own food. They bought what they could afford from the gaolers. Otherwise they subsisted on charity and sometimes were allowed into the streets, in chained gangs, to beg for their bread; but prisoners awaiting death were supplied with a minimum of food by the magistrates. It was small wonder, therefore, that prisoners with a little money were only too thankful if they found judges who were open to bribery. These 'trading justices', whom Smollett described as of 'profligate lives, needy, mean, ignorant and rapacious', managed to bribe their way into office and many made handsome livings.

The system of voluntary constables had also broken down, for men often delegated their duties to those who were prepared to do the work for them, for a small payment. In London, however, since the time of Charles II, a small force of paid watchmen – the Charlies – had been established, but they were mostly frail old men, unfit for any other kind of work, and, being armed only with long staves, were useless against any armed aggressor, let alone the strong and well-armed criminals who were now roaming the streets.

William Shenstone, writing in the first half of the century, said: 'London is really dangerous at this time; the pickpockets, formerly content with mere filching, make no scruple to knock people down with bludgeons in Fleet Street and the Strand, and that at no later hour than eight o'clock at night; but in the Piazzas, Covent Garden, they come in large bodies, armed with couteaus, and attack whole parties, so that the danger of coming out of the playhouses is of some weight in the opposite scale when I am disposed to go to them oftener than I ought.'

This was the state of London when John Gay arrived. Born in Devon in 1685, and left fatherless by the time he was ten, he was sent to London to be apprenticed to a silk mercer, but he hated the work and after a few years managed to get a discharge from his master and devote himself to writing. He published his first poems with only moderate success but became a friend of Pope and through his influence was appointed domestic secretary to the Duchess of Monmouth. His early plays were as unsuccessful as his poems, but in 1715 he published his *Trivia*: or *The Art of Walking the Streets of London*, and of Drury Lane, once so elegant, he wrote:

Oh! may thy virtues guard thee through the roads
Of Drury's mazy courts and dark abodes,
The Harlot's guileful paths, who nightly stand
Where Katherine Street descends into the Strand.

His fortunes were still only moderate during George I's time. With the accession of George II, he was offered the post of gentleman-usher to the three-year-old Princess Louisa, but although ambitious for a Court appointment, he considered this beneath his consideration and rejected it. Pope introduced him to Dean Swift, who suggested he wrote a Newgate pastoral in which the characters should be thieves and highwaymen. The idea appealed to Gay, and he wrote *The Beggar's Opera*, which he began as a satire on the much criticized Italian opera. He offered it to Drury Lane, but they rejected it. At Lincoln's Inn, Christopher Rich had died, but his son, John, had taken over the management of the theatre, and when Gay showed him the opera, he accepted it. It was produced in 1727 and was an immediate success.

Theatres at this time were run as repertories, the usual run of a play, if successful, being nine days, when the author received the receipts of three performances. But *The Beggar's Opera* ran for an unprecedented sixty-two nights, and the following season it was produced throughout the country, at Bath and Bristol and in both Wales and Scotland.

John Rich made a lot of money, and now, to the consternation of the Drury Lane lessees, he issued a prospectus, inviting people to take shares in a new theatre which he proposed to build in Bow Street, on land leased from the Duke of Bedford. £6,000 was soon subscribed and building began. His theatre went up behind some of the Bow Street houses, one entrance being approached by a narrow passage between two of the houses, but the grand entrance was in the north-east corner of the piazza. It was a beautiful theatre, designed by James Shepherd, with a seating capacity of about two thousand – similar to that of Drury Lane.

It meant that among the people of the crowded market-place – the greengrocers and flower-sellers, the tavern-keepers and proprietors of the coffee-houses, the quack doctors and fortune-tellers, the panders and prostitutes – came ever more players and their admirers; and whatever the varying fortunes of the theatres might be, the market flourished as never before.

Rich used Davenant's royal patent, which had been granted by Charles II, for there was still a monopoly on the running of theatres in England, although it was not rigidly observed. Nevertheless, it was not until early in the nineteenth century, when the patent law was ended, that people were legally free to open theatres for any kind of entertainment they wished.

He opened on 7 December 1732, with Congreve's comedy *The Way of the World*. For John Rich, whose father had been so ignominiously turned away from Drury Lane, the return to Covent Garden was a triumph, and Hogarth's cartoon 'Rich's Glory', shows his exultant arrival from Lincoln's Inn Fields.

'The cloathes, scenes and decorations entirely new, and, on account of the great demand for places, the pit and boxes, by desire, will be laid together at 5/-; gallery 2/-; upper gallery 1s; and to prevent the scenes being crowded, the stage half-a-guinea. N.B. all persons who want places are desired to send to the stage door (the passage from Bow Street leading to it), where attendance will be given and places kept for the following nights as usual,' ran his advertisement.

From the outset, the shows in the new theatre were more spectacular and lavish than those at Drury Lane, particularly the pantomimes, for which John Rich, himself an actor of no mean talents, had created the part of Harlequin.

John Rich was a pleasant, amusing man, and eminent visitors often dropped in to his private room at the theatre, to chat with him and his scene-painter, Lambert. One evening, when Rich was grilling a steak for his supper, a visitor called, and Rich invited him to share it with him, accompanied by a bottle of port 'from the tavern close by'. It was so good that others soon joined them, and by 1735 the 'Sublime Society of Beefsteaks' was established, which was to last for more than a century.

The number of members was limited to twenty-four, and over the years it included George, Prince of Wales, with his brothers the Dukes of York and Sussex, Sheridan, Garrick, John Wilkes, the Duke of Argyll and the Duke of Leinster. They used to meet on Saturday nights throughout the winter months, but 'they abhor the notion of being thought a club,' wrote Peter Cunningham. 'They dedicate their hours to "Beef and Liberty" and enjoy a hearty English dinner with hearty English appetites.'

George II had appointed Handel Court musician, and his oratorio *Esther*, the first ever to be heard in England, had been performed at the King's theatre in the Haymarket in 1732, but he ran into difficulties with the management and it was at Rich's theatre that his next works were heard, Rich being always ready to present new forms of entertainment. Handel's *Ariodante* and *Alcina* both had their premières at Covent Garden during the 1730s, and amongst his singers were Rich's son-in-law, John Beard, Cecilia Young, who was to marry Thomas Arne, and Arne's sister, Mrs Cibber.

Handel presented three new oratorios, *Alexander's Feast*, *Acis and Galatea* and *Esther*, all of which were triumphantly successful. For these, as for his operas, admission charges were raised. Writing of the performance of *Alexander's Feast*, the *Daily Post* reported: 'There never was, upon like occasion, so numerous and splendid an audience at any theatre in London, there being at least 1,300 persons present, and it is judged that the receipts of the House could not amount to less than £450.' During Lent, Covent Garden gave concerts of sacred music, for which Handel composed *Samson, Judas Maccabeus* and *Solomon*; and then, in 1741, came the greatest of them all, the *Messiah*.

The Italian opera-house continued to play, but to dwindling audiences, and the Court and nobility were divided into two factions, the King and Queen still visiting the Haymarket, while the opposing faction, disliking Italian opera, set up those more to their taste at the Lincoln's Inn theatre, which they leased from Rich.

At Covent Garden, Rich's star actor was James Quin, and he soon found the young Peg Woffington, who first appeared there in 1738, beginning a brilliant but tempestuous stage career of nearly twenty years. One of her bitterest rivals was the beautiful George Anne Bellamy. On one occasion she had 'procured from Paris two gorgeous dresses wherein to enact Statira in The Rival Queens. Rozana was played by Peg Woffington, and she was so overcome with malice when she saw herself eclipsed by the dazzling glories of the resplendent Bellamy, that she rolled Statira and her spangled sack in the dust, pommelling her the while with the handle of her stage dagger, as she declaimed, Alexander standing by:

Nor he, nor heaven shall shield thee from my justice!
Die, sorceress, die! and all my wrongs die with thee!'

George Anne Bellamy was the illegitimate daughter of an Irish peer, and Rich, mainly for the sake of her mother, gave the girl her first chance on the stage when she was only about fourteen. She was at once successful, and Quin, catching her in his arms as she left the stage on her first night, exclaimed: 'Thou art a divine creature and the true spirit is in thee.'

She loved clothes and spent a large proportion of her salary on the best that Paris could offer. As she says in her biography, she had a figure 'not inelegant, a powerful voice, inexhaustible spirits and some humour', while her benefit nights were 'lucrative to an excess', and whether or not she was a great actress, she was immensely popular for a time and much sought after by a succession of suitors, being for a time the mistress of Charles James Fox.

With the retirement of Colley Cibber from Drury Lane, the management came, after several manoeuvres, into the hands of

Charles Fleetwood, and amongst his company was a young actress, Kitty Clive, and a hot-tempered Irishman, Charles Macklin, as well as James Quin, who left the Covent Garden theatre to join them. But although Quin was considered to be the finest actor on the London stage, and a worthy successor to Barton Booth, his acting was still in the old tradition, with speeches declaimed in grave sonority, deep and rich but monotonous. It was Macklin who at last broke away from the old, mannered interpretation and established a new conception of the actor's function. He first showed his originality with a new portrayal of Shylock, a part which hitherto had always been played by the comedian, who had contrived to make him a figure of fun. Macklin portrayed him as mean, then pathetic and, in the end, tragic; as Pope said:

This is the Jew
That Shakespeare knew.

The warm-hearted but temperamental Kitty Clive played Portia to Macklin's Shylock, and the other star actress at Drury Lane was Mrs Pritchard, famous for her Lady Macbeth, for which, like all tragediennes, she wore long black gloves with her eighteenth-century Court dress.

6

Vagabonds and Players

It was in 1729, only two years after Rich had opened the Covent Garden theatre, that Colonel Thomas de Veil was appointed Justice of the Peace for Middlesex and Westminster. He was a man of proved integrity, both during his years in the army and later as a businessman, and he took his new appointment very seriously. Before accepting it, he studied the powers and duties that would be assigned to him, and it very soon became clear that he was more interested in combating crime in London than in the welfare of the criminals. Moreover, he soon proved to be a very able detective himself, and within the first few months of taking office he had discovered the leaders of one particularly vicious gang which had been haunting Covent Garden and the Strand for months. The gang became so nervous that they attempted to waylay and murder him, but the Colonel was too quick for them, and they were soon all brought to retribution.

Colonel Veil first lived in Soho, but after a few years he moved to a house in Bow Street, from where he administered his office. In 1744 the footmen of London organized a protest against the unfair competition they were suffering from French footmen, and for their first meeting they hired a room in Panton Street. The Government asked Colonel de Veil to prevent the meeting, and when the footmen arrived at Panton Street, they found the door locked. The proprietor, in order to get rid of them, said that Colonel de Veil had taken the key away, whereupon the angry crowd, two or three hundred strong, swarmed along to Bow Street to demand it. It happened that the Colonel did not have the key, but they refused to believe him. Neighbours sent for help, but before the soldiers arrived, the infuriated waiters broke all the windows and then smashed down the front door. With the Colonel standing on the stairs, to protect his wife and children who had fled upstairs, they rampaged through the ground floor and broke up all the furniture. When the soldiers at last arrived, there was a battle royal until the men were eventually overcome. A few weeks later, the Colonel received a knighthood.

In 1737, while de Veil was still in office, Dr Johnson and David Garrick arrived in London from Lichfield, Garrick, after attending the local grammar school, having been a pupil of Samuel Johnson at his short-lived academy, which had dismally failed. Johnson was twenty-eight and Garrick twenty. They were both poor, and both had come south to seek their fortune.

Johnson took a room in the house of a staymaker in Exeter Street, Covent Garden, where he subsisted on 4½d a day until he obtained work with Edward Cave, who had launched his *Gentleman's Magazine* in a room in the old gateway of the ruined Clerkenwell Priory. Then he was able to record: 'I dined very well for eightpence, with very good company, at the Pine Apple in New Street. Several of them had travelled. They expected to meet every day, but did not know each other's names. It used to cost the others a shilling, for they drank wine; but I had a cut of meat for sixpence, and bread for a penny, and gave the waiter a penny; so that I was quite well served, aye! better than they, for they gave the waiter nothing.'

And it was he who recorded one of the few ghost stories about Covent Garden. It concerned his cousin, the Reverend Mr Ford, 'a man in whom both talents and good disposition were disgraced by licentiousness, but who was a very able judge of what was right'. The story goes that a waiter at the Hummums, where Ford died, 'had been absent for some time, and returned, not knowing that Ford was dead. Going down to the cellar, he met him; going down again, he met him a second time. When he came up, he asked some of the people of the house what Ford could be doing there. They told him Ford was dead. The waiter took a fever, in which he lay for some time. When he recovered, he said he had a message to deliver to some women for Ford; but he was not allowed to tell what or to whom. He walked out; he was followed; but somewhere about St Paul's they lost him. He came back, and said he had delivered the message, and the women had exclaimed, "Then we are all undone." '

'Dr Pelleter, who was not a credulous man,' says Boswell, 'inquired into the truth of the story, and he said the evidence was irresistible ... To be sure, the man had a fever; and the vision may have been the beginning of it. But if the message to the women, and their behaviour upon it, were true as related, there was something supernatural. That rests upon his word; and there it remains.'

David Garrick, on arriving in London, became a student at Lincoln's Inn for about a year, but then he inherited £1,000 from an uncle who had been in the wine trade in Lisbon. His father was dead, but after a return to Lichfield to discuss affairs with his elder brother Peter, who had also received a legacy, they decided to set up in the wine trade themselves, Peter to remain in Lichfield and David to act as the London representative. He established himself in an office in Durham Yard, off the Strand, and was soon selling his wine to the actors who met at the Bedford Coffee House in the piazza.

Garrick's heart had always been in acting, and he spent a great deal of time at the theatres. He was a small man – only five feet four inches – but very attractive, warm-hearted and lively, with a wonderful gift for mimicry, and soon he had struck up a warm friendship with Macklin, a regular member of the Bedford Coffee House circle.

Johnson arranged for him to take part in an amateur performance of Fielding's *Mock Doctor* at Cave's office at Clerkenwell. Garrick took the lead, and several of the printers took minor parts, including young Hogarth, who kept on forgetting his lines. Through Johnson's influence, Garrick began contributing play criticisms to the *Gentleman's Magazine*, and also to write his own first plays. He applied to both Fleetwood at Drury Lane and Rich at Covent Garden for stage work, but they both rejected him. But at last he was given the part of Richard III at a new and as yet unlicensed theatre in Goodman's Fields, down in the city near Aldgate. He was an outstanding success, and the next morning the *Daily Post* reported that his reception had been 'the most extraordinary and great that was ever known', while *The Champion* wrote of his voice, saying that it was 'neither whining, bellowing, nor grumbling, but perfectly easy in its transitions, natural in its cadence, and beautiful in its elocution', and went on to record that 'he is not less happy in his mien and gait, in which he is neither strutting nor mincing, neither stiff nor slouching. When three or four are on the stage with him, he is attentive to whatever is spoke, and never drops his characters when he has finished a speech by either looking contemptuously on an inferior performer, unnecessary spitting, or suffering his eyes to wander through the whole circle of spectators. His action is never superfluous, awkward, or too frequently repeated, but graceful, decent and becoming.'

All of which is interesting, not only as an estimate of Garrick's acting but as an indication of how some of the older hands conducted themselves on the stage.

At first, since the stage was still considered a barely respectable profession for men, let alone women, he appeared under an assumed name, but for his first benefit night at Goodman's Fields he declared himself as Richard Sheridan and quickly became popular and socially accepted by the theatre-goers in London society, dining frequently with many of their distinguished members, including Lord Halifax and Lord Chesterfield.

After a second season at Goodman's Fields the theatre was closed and the licence not renewed, Giffard, the manager, going with his wife to the Lincoln's Inn theatre; but Fleetwood now gave Sheridan a contract to play at Drury Lane for the following season, at a fee of 600 guineas, and here he joined the company of Macklin, Kitty Clive and Mrs Pritchard. They protested at his restlessness, his pace and his new ways on the stage, but his power over the audience was undeniable. 'If this young fellow be right, then *we* have all been wrong,' admitted Quin at last.

Peg Woffington joined the company, leaving Covent Garden, and was Macklin's mistress for a while. But then she and Garrick fell in love. She was twenty-four and Garrick twenty-five, and they lived together for a time at Number 6 Bow Street, next door but one to the theatre, a house which had been built by Wilkes, the actor.

Fleetwood, increasingly crippled with gout, made money at Drury Lane but took to gambling and general dissipation. He borrowed heavily and mortgaged the theatre. Salaries were unpaid and soon the bailiffs arrived. The actors met at the end of the summer of 1743 and appointed Lacy, the comedian, as their new manager. Fleetwood fled to France, selling his patent to Green and Amber for £3,200, and they confirmed Lacy as their manager, with a third of the profits. In 1745 Lacy asked Garrick to join him in part managership, but at the time he was not interested, having been invited to play at Covent Garden by Rich, along with Mrs Cibber and Quin. This was the year of the '45 Highland invasion. As the Young Pretender advanced southwards, during the first few days of the rebellion, there was a run on the Bank of England, and Green and Amber failed. Lacy appealed again to Garrick, and this time he agreed to join him at Drury Lane, it being arranged that Lacy would be in charge of the wardrobe and scenery, as well as the money affairs, while Garrick was to deal with authors, engage the players and superintend rehearsals.

They opened together in 1747, by which time Garrick had quarrelled with Peg Woffington, because, it was said, of her extravagance, and had moved to a lodging in King Street.

Garrick's style of acting was different from anything that had ever been seen on the stage before. He always wore high heels, because he was so short, but he moved well and had an extremely expressive face. His aim, like Macklin's, was to free acting from the restraints which long traditions had imposed, particularly in the interpretation of classical roles, but he went further and deeper than Macklin, studying his characters with sympathy and understanding, identifying himself with them, suffering their pain and tragedy, living in their emotions of joy and love, agony, fear and remorse. He had the gift of empathy, which involves both the emotions and the intellect, and was able to take on the very essence of the personalities of his parts. This was the secret of Garrick's genius and the reason that he was acclaimed as greater even than Betterton.

Describing a performance of *The Fair Penitent*, a critic said that Quin appeared as Horatio, wearing an enormous periwig, rolled stockings and high-heeled, square-toed shoes, and that he spoke in 'deep, full tones, with little variation in cadence, accompanied by a sawing kind of action which had more of the senate than of the stage in it, rolling out heroics with an air of dignified indifference'. Mrs Cibber, at Calista, spoke in a voice which was 'so extremely wanting in contrast, that thought it did not wound the ear, it wearied it', but 'when little Garrick bounced on the stage it seemed as if a whole century had been swept over in the transition of a single scene; old things were done away and a new order at once brought forward, bright and luminous, and clearly destined to dispel the barbarisms and bigotry of a tasteless age, too long attached to the prejudices of custom and superstitiously devoted to the illusion of imposing declamation.'

This writer was kinder to Mrs Pritchard than Dr Johnson, who once remarked: 'It is wonderful how little mind she has.'

For all his artistry, Garrick did not yet adopt realism in stage costume, declaring that the audiences would never accept it. He played Lear in eighteenth-century breeches, white shirt and ermine-trimmed coat, Macbeth in a scarlet coat, silver-laced waistcoat and eighteenth-century wig and breeches, and Hotspur in a laced frock and Ramillies wig.

The salaries of the actresses included a liberal allowance for their clothes. Mrs Yates, for example, asked Garrick for £700 salary and £200 for her clothes. 'Considering my novelty, to say nothing of my beauty, I think I cannot in conscience take less,' she said, 'as I love to be well dressed, and the characters I appear in require it.' In the end they settled for £800. For Mrs Cibber, all her clothes were found for her except her head-dresses – and this was the period of monstrously high head-dresses – an absurd fashion which began after the end of the Seven Years War, when Englishwomen began visiting Paris again.

Hair was piled on top of the head over large wire frames stuffed with tow, wool and hemp. The whole erection was then well greased and dusted with grey or white powder and decorated with flowers and feathers, while enormous false curls were fixed on either side of the face. Skirts became as cumbersome as the head-dresses, draped over circular hoops stiffened with whalebone, which with the passing years grew ever larger, and whalebone was also used to stiffen their truly formidable corsets.

George Anne Bellamy seems to have spent more than any of the other actresses on her clothes, and when she was playing Cordelia at Drury Lane in the presence of George II, she was mortified to overhear his reply to the Lord Chamberlain, who had asked him what he thought of her performance: 'Umph! very well, but her hoop is so large.' It was an echo of James I's complaint, more than a century and a half earlier, that the fashion for farthingales was ridiculous. 'The impertinent garment takes up all the room,' he grumbled, and tried, though in vain, to forbid their being worn at Court.

Actresses sometimes bought the cast-off dresses of society women, and George Anne Bellamy once wore for her part of Cleopatra a dress of silver tissue which the Princess of Wales had worn only once, for a royal christening, and discarded.

There were certain conventions about stage clothes, however. Older actresses always wore black velvet, young girls white satin, while murderers always had their faces chalked and wore black periwigs. 'Gentleman' Smith complained of the shabbiness of his Richard II's hat, and asked for the one Powell had worn as King John; Hale, as Charles I, insisted on wearing a full-bottomed wig, but Henderson, less concerned about appearance, boasted of having played ten characters in one season in the same dress.

Scenery was just as conventional and unrealistic, and new plays seldom had anything but a selection of the six stock sets – a street, a bedroom, a parlour, a hall, a park with trees and a garden, and action had to be fitted into whichever suited it best.

Much to the disappointment of several of the actresses, particularly Mrs Cibber, after his second season in management at Drury Lane, Garrick made a very happy marriage with Eva Violette, a young dancer.

Her parentage was something of a mystery, but it was generally thought that she was the illegitimate daughter of the Earl of Burlington by an aristocratic young Florentine and that, when her mother died and the Earl's agent mishandled the allowance that should have been paid to the young girl, she was forced to earn a living by her dancing. But she was no ordinary dancer and performed at the Court of Vienna before coming to London. She was then twenty-one and stayed at Burlington House with the Earl and Countess, and their daughter Georgina, who was to become the Duchess of Devonshire. Eva continued dancing in London professionally for a time, although carefully chaperoned. She performed both at the Haymarket theatre and at Drury Lane, where she and Garrick fell deeply in love. And with the Earl's blessing, they were married in 1749, setting up house at 27 Southampton Street, which remained their London home for the next twenty-three years, until they moved to the newly built Adelphi.

This was the year that Garrick produced Dr Johnson's play *Irene*. Garrick ran into a lot of trouble with it, because he wanted alterations which at first Johnson would not permit. Only after a violent argument would he at last allow some of the changes to be made, although still they were not enough. Dr Adams was present at the first night and gave Boswell the following account. 'Before the curtain drew up, there were catcalls and whistling, which alarmed Johnson's friends. The Prologue, which was written by himself in a manly strain, soothed the audience, and the play went off tolerably well till it came to the conclusion, when Mrs Pritchard, the Heroine of the piece, was to be strangled upon the stage, and was to speak two lines with the bow-string round her neck. The audience cried out "Murder! Murder!" She several times attempted to speak; but in vain. At last she was obliged to go off the stage alive.'

'This passage,' says Boswell, 'was afterwards struck out, and she was carried behind the scenes, as the play now has it ...

'Notwithstanding all the support of such performers as Garrick, Barry, Mrs Cibber, Mrs Pritchard, and every advantage of dress and decoration, the tragedy did not please the public. Mr Garrick's zeal carried it through for nine nights, so that the author had his three nights' profits; ... and Mr Robert Dodsley gave him £100 for the copy, with his usual reservation of the right of one edition.'

Macklin was growing old, and in 1754 he retired from the stage to set up a coffee-house of his own – the Piazza – in the north-east corner of the square, perhaps hoping to rival the popular Bedford, meeting-place of the younger actors, whose success, particularly that of Garrick, he found difficult to accept. His new public ordinary, he announced, would be served each day at four o'clock, for 3 shillings, which included port, claret or any other liquor. Poor Macklin had big ideas which did not work. As the clock struck four each day, a bell rang for five minutes and the order was given to the kitchen to serve the meal. Ten minutes later it was on the table, and the doors were closed to any other visitors. Macklin himself, in full dress suit, always carried in the first dish, and when he had set it before his guests, he retired to the sideboard, to keep a watchful eye on his waiters, who had been instructed to make no sound as they worked, so that the guests' enjoyment should not in any way be impaired. Macklin strove to feed his clients' souls and minds, as well as their bodies, for he announced a series of after-dinner debates on the arts, sciences, literature, criticism, philosophy, history, politics and morality. He announced that, 'Mr Macklin intends to lecture upon the comedy of the ancients, the use of their masks and flutes, their mimes and pantomimes, and the use and abuse of the stage. He will likewise lecture on the rise and progress of modern theatres, making a comparison between them and those of Greece and Rome, and between each other; he also proposes to lecture upon each of Shakespeare's plays.'

It was not to be, for nobody wanted to hear him. Nine months later, Macklin was bankrupt and returned to the stage, but the Piazza Coffee House, passing into other hands, began to prosper, and in the years to come became a favourite resort of Sheridan and Kemble.

Garrick served Drury Lane well. He brought order to the stage. He cleared away the stage boxes and excluded the members of the audience who had been in the habit of sitting on the stage in front of them, sometimes in such large numbers that the players had scarcely room to move. On one occasion, old Quin, playing Falstaff, took several minutes to work his way to the front of the stage through the crowd of young men and women who wedged him in, while on another occasion Mrs Cibber, in Juliet's white satin dress with its large 'banging' hoop, found she could hardly turn round, she was so 'encompassed around'.

On their benefit nights, the players had tended to encourage this practice and arranged accomodation for their supporters at the back of the stage with 5-shilling seats, although at least one actor, Tate Wilkinson, objected, describing them as 'horrid intrusions on the mind of sensibility'.

Garrick put a stop to all this and provided more seats in the auditorium. He made many practical improvements, particularly in regard to lighting, and appointed Dr Arne as musical director, although a few years later Arne moved to Covent Garden. He insisted on regular, punctual rehearsals and inspired his players with his own spirit of naturalism; and at last he began a few dress reforms which were later to develop into stage realism.

Choosing which plays to present was no light task, although he was inundated with scripts from hopeful writers, many of them clergymen and some of them young rakes hoping, as a last resort, that a success at Drury Lane might recoup their fortunes. They all pressed him to perform their work, 'some known to famine, some to fame'. Rich suffered from these would-be playwrights as much as Garrick, and in Hogarth's picture of the Rake, nearly at the end of his Progress, he is carrying a letter from Rich with the gloomy words: 'Sr I have read yr Play, and find it will not doe.'

Garrick wrote to Dr Arne: 'I have read your play and rode your horse, and do not approve of either,' and on his copy of the letter he noted: 'Designed for Dr Arne, who sold me a horse, a very dull one; and sent me a comic opera, ditto', while of Dr Johnson's dialogue he said that all his women characters spoke like Johnsons in petticoats.

All of them seemed to take it as a personal affront when he rejected their manuscripts, and of those he accepted, he often made drastic alterations, as he did even to Shakespeare, sometimes, it was alleged, to improve, as he thought, his own parts.

The trouble was that there was no outstanding dramatist during these middle years of the eighteenth century, until Oliver Goldsmith arrived with his play *The Good-Natur'd Man*, which Garrick rejected but which was produced at Covent Garden in 1763.

It was about this time that Garrick introduced the Drury Lane pantomime each Christmas and that Mrs Cibber became one of his most distinguished actresses. She had begun her career as a singer, and Handel had been a great admirer of her voice, having written the part of Galatea for her in his *Acis and Galatea*, and also some of the arias in the *Messiah*, but she grew tired of opera and oratorio, or may have felt that her singing voice was past its prime, and came to Drury Lane to act with Garrick.

There was keen rivalry now between the two theatres, and they both had troubles and tragedies. In 1757 the beautiful Peg Woffington, playing her favourite part of Rosalind in *As You Like It*, suffered a stroke and had to be carried from the stage. It was her final exit, for she was never to play again. She was only forty-four, and four years later she died. The next year Theophilus Cibber, Mrs Cibber's husband, was drowned on his way to play at Dublin; and in 1761 John Rich died. His son-in-law, John Beard, the tenor, took over the management for the production of Arne's lyric operas, of which the best known are *Thomas and Sally*, *Artaxerxes* and *Love in a Village*.

Despite the elegance of the theatre and the quality of the presentations, the eighteenth-century gallery audiences were as boisterous and ill-behaved here as at the Lane. A visiting Frenchman reported, in 1763, that there was 'a great deal of barking and howling and throwing of orange peel at a man whose face displeased the gallery. The gallery controlled the acting and thanked the players.'

When *Artaxerxes* was presented, the production was so costly that the management decided to raise admission prices, but the audience showed their resentment in no uncertain manner. 'A riot happened at Covent Garden theatre occasioned by a demand being made for full prices at the opera of ARTAXERXES,' ran the Press report. 'The mischief done was the greatest ever known on any occasion of the like kind; all the benches of the boxes and pit being entirely torn to pieces. The rashness of the rioters was so great that they cut away the wooden pillars between the boxes, so that if the inside of them had not been iron, they would have brought the galleries down upon their heads. The damages done amount to at least £2000. Four persons concern'd in the riots have been committed to the Gatehouse.'

Five years after the production of *The Good-Natur'd Man*, Goldsmith's *She Stoops to Conquer* was produced at Covent Garden, but by this time Beard had sold his patent, and after a year or two of manoeuvring, Thomas Harris had become sole manager of the theatre.

Harris now presented Italian operas by contemporary composers, as well as plays, and after a performance of Tarchi's *La Generosità d'Alessandro*, the *Morning Post* reported that Marchsesi, the male soprano, had never sung to better effect, but the 'leading soprano, Giuliani, was chiefly distinguished for the very disgusting mode of rolling her eyes and distorting her features'.

By now both Quin and Mrs Cibber were dead and Kitty Clive had retired to Strawberry Hill, where she lived for many more years, enjoying the company of her friend Horace Walpole and his literary circle, but the ageing Macklin stayed on at the theatre for years. His last performance was not until 1789, by which time he was well into his nineties and his power and his memory had all gone. Old and feeble, he attempted to play his famous role of Shylock for his benefit, but he forgot his lines, broke down and had to be led from the stage. Even so, he lived on for another ten years, in his lodgings in Covent Garden, wandering about the piazza and haunting the theatre where he had achieved so many triumphs.

Kitty Clive's old rival, George Anne Bellamy, had a tragic end. She went on acting until she was well into her sixties, and then, in 1784, crippled with gout, she had to retire, but she was hopelessly in debt and at last was taken to the King's Bench prison. None of her old lovers came to help her, and even her own son did nothing, for he now had a mistress of his own, who forbade it.

She sold all her clothes and jewellery and was eventually released from prison, but she was now almost penniless. In her *Memoirs* she described walking alone into St George's Fields, 'not without the hope of meeting some freebooters who frequented these lawless parts, and who would take away the life of which I was so weary'. Then she made her way to the steps of Westminster Bridge, thinking to drown herself, but she changed her mind when she came across a woman with a child, who was in even more desperate straits than herself. With her last few shillings, she took a dingy little room in Lambeth, and here, in 1788, alone and in dire and sordid poverty, she died.

At the Bow Street Police Office, Sir Thomas de Veil had died in 1748, and through the influence of the Duke of Bedford, Henry Fielding was appointed to succeed him. Fielding had already written a few plays, and although one or two had been produced, they had not met with any great success. Now he settled down with his family in the Bow Street house, and living with them was his blind half-brother John.

Like Sir Thomas de Veil, Henry Fielding took his new appointment seriously and was soon hard at work. By the end of his first year in office, his band of constables, were, as usual, due for retirement, but he persuaded some of them to stay on, for a small remuneration. These men were the beginning of the Bow Street police force, and within the next year he had eighty constables under his command, for whom he drew up a code of conduct; but he did not have the money available to keep the men on any longer, and this first force had to be disbanded.

It was now, in 1749, that Fielding's masterpiece was published, *The History of Tom Jones, A Foundling*, on which he had been working for many years. He began the short-lived *Covent Garden Journal*, in which he published accounts of many of the cases which came before him; and he continued Sir John de Veil's conduct of careful investigation and strict fairness in his judgements.

Yet crime did not abate, and the Government realized that something must be done about it. The Gin Act of 1751, the Act for 'the Better Preventing of Thefts and Robberies and for Regulating Places of Public Entertainment and Punishing Persons Keeping Disorderly Houses', not to mention the Act for 'Preventing the Horrid Crime of Murder', in which there was a warning that condemned men should have only bread and water, and no alcoholic drink before their execution, barely touched the problem, for there was still no machinery for enforcing them, while promises of rewards for information were of little avail, since most people were too frightened to come forward and tell all they knew.

In 1751 Fielding published his novel *Amelia* and also an important pamphlet, *Enquiry into the Increase of Robbers*, which moved the government at last, thoroughly alarmed at the worsening crime rate in London, to accept his plan to establish a paid force of constables. But his health was failing rapidly, and already his blind brother John was helping him and becoming as deeply involved in the work.

In 1754 Henry was obliged to resign office. He undertook the journey to Lisbon, hoping to recover his health, but two months later he died, while John, who was shortly afterwards knighted, took the oath for Middlesex and Westminster and administered the new Bow Street runners.

At first there were only six, but they were men with special skill in solving crimes, and they were prepared to travel anywhere in the country, or even abroad, if it were necessary. In addition to this 'special branch', Sir John had a patrol of sixty-eight men based on the Bow Street office. They were divided into thirteen parties, each comprising an officer and three or four men, and they patrolled the streets at night and at other times when there were large gatherings which might break into disorder. They were all armed with cutlasses, and the officers also carried a brace of pistols. They did not wear a special uniform yet, and it was not until early in the nineteenth century that they were put into dark blue coats and trousers, red waistcoats and black leather hats, and were known as 'the Robin Redbreasts'.

In the *Gentleman's Magazine* for 15 September 1775, it was reported: 'This day, Sir John Fielding informed the bench of justices that he had last year written to Mr Garrick concerning the impropriety of performing THE BEGGAR'S OPERA, which never was represented on the stage without creating an additional number of real thieves; he begged, therefore, the gentlemen present would join him in requesting Mr Garrick to desist from performing that opera on Saturday evening. The bench immediately consented to the proposal; and a polite card was despatched to Mr Garrick for that purpose. To which Mr Garrick returned for answer, that his company was so imperfect and divided (many of the performers being yet in the country), that it would be exceedingly inconvenient, if not impossible, for him to open with any other piece than that he had already advertised; but added that he would, in future, do everything in his power to oblige them.'

Although *The Beggar's Opera* had been so successful during the fifty years since it had first been produced, and had been revived often, it had always provoked the kind of criticism that Sir John Fielding expressed. It was much on the lines of Seneca's assertion in regard to the daily manuscript paper which was circulated in Roman times. 'Not a gazette,' he said, 'without its divorce, so that our matrons, from constantly hearing of them, soon learn to follow the example.'

When, inspired by *The Beggar's Opera*, a play was produced a few years later, about Jack Shepherd, the highwayman, the Lord Chamberlain had decided that the glorification of a criminal was so bad for the morals of the younger generation that he had forbidden its presentation.

Kitty Clive declared that *The Beggar's Opera* was a most harmful play, and Edmund Burke said that 'the spirit that would treat crime with levity' was 'disastrous to good citizenship'. William Hazlitt, on the other hand, said he thought the play had done more towards putting down highway robbery than all the gibbets ever erected.

These are the two opposite points of view that are still being argued, now that violence and crime are presented on the television screens every day of the week. Most of the plays still preserve the convention that crime does not pay in the end and that the criminal ultimately receives a just retribution, so it is impossible to say how many people, with criminal tendencies, are warned in time and deterred through fear of the consequences, if for no moral reason; but no one can deny that today numbers of young criminals who find themselves in the dock have pleaded that they copied the idea for their crimes from something they had seen on the television screen. Moreover, as crime increases every year, so, in a horrifying crescendo, does the amount of material for them to copy appear on the screens; and it is a sobering thought that the warning of the evil influence of the portrayal of a bad example should have been given to the world so early.

The three great eighteenth-century English artists William Hogarth, Richard Wilson and Sir Joshua Reynolds were all associated with Covent Garden.

Hogarth, said E.V. Lucas, was not only 'the first great national British painter, the first man to look at the English life around him like an Englishman and paint it without affectation or foreign influence, but he was the first to make pictures popular. Hogarth's engravings from his own work produced a love of art that has steadily increased ever since.'

He was born in Smithfield in 1697 and was first apprenticed to a silversmith near Leicester Fields, but by the time he was twenty-one he had set up as an engraver on his own account. At the same time, he attended Sir James Thornhill's academy in the piazza. They did not get on particularly well, for Hogarth disliked Thornhill's insistence on copying other men's pictures. 'It is like pouring water out of one vessel into another,' he said. He preferred to see the world through his own eyes, and it is by his work that we have been given so clear a picture of what Covent Garden was like during the early eighteenth century. Another reason for Thornhill's doubts about Hogarth was that the young man fell in love with his daughter, Jane, for whom he was not considered to be a good enough match. In the end they eloped, but a few years later, when Hogarth had achieved his first real success, with the pictures he drew of scenes from *The Beggar's Opera*, he and Thornhill were reconciled.

Hogarth did some brilliant portraits, not of the aristocracy but of the ordinary folk he met in and around Covent Garden, but his main source of income was from his engravings of his narrative pictures of life as he saw it, the most well known of all being *The Rake's Progress* and *Marriage à la Mode*, which he exhibited at Cock's auction rooms in the piazza, where later the Tavistock Hotel was established.

He was one of the company which frequented the Bedford Coffee House, as well as being one of the original members of the Beefsteak Club.

Richard Wilson's story was sadly different. He was born in 1714 and came to London as a portrait painter, setting up his studio in the piazza. In 1748 he was commissioned to paint the Prince of Wales and the Duke of York, and with the money he earned from this work he paid a visit to Italy, where he developed his true love, which was landscape painting. Here again he was very successful and when he returned to Covent Garden a few years later, in 1756, it seemed at first that his success would continue, but English taste had not yet come to appreciate his individual style of landscape painting, with his flaming sunsets and cloud-shadowed skies, and he soon found difficulty in selling his work, except to one or two enlightened patrons.

By taking pupils and painting English landscapes, as well as more portraits, including a splendid one of Peg Woffington, he managed to make a tolerable living, and when the Royal Academy was established, in 1768, with Sir Joshua Reynolds as its first president, George III nominated him as one of the founder members, and he also became its librarian, but he was making little money from his landscapes and becoming increasingly disappointed and bitter. Then, through an argument with Lord Bute over the price of one of his paintings which the King had a mind to buy and which Bute, as the intermediary, said was too high, poor Wilson lost favour at Court. His former patrons and his fellow academicians avoided him, and with only the £50 a year from his librarianship on which to live, he had to move to a miserable attic in Tottenham Street, off the Tottenham Court Road, 'living on bread and an excess of porter, although it was lack of food rather than an excess of drink which destroyed him'. In the end he was befriended by some of his Welsh relations and taken to spend his last year or two at Llanberis, where he died in 1782.

And Peter Pindar wrote the wise prediction:

But, honest Wilson, never mind; ...
Wait till thou hast been dead a hundred year.

Today Wilson is regarded as our first truly great landscape artist, but amongst his Italian landscapes which are so treasured today are some which at one time belonged to a director of the East India Company and which were discovered after the owner's death 'covered with dust and piled together in a heap, against the wall of a miserable garret'.

At the time of his death, William Turner, whose wonderful landscapes were to be in the Wilson tradition, was growing up in Covent Garden, for he was born in 1775, at his father's barber's shop, Number 26, Maiden Lane.

Joshua Reynolds was nine years younger than Wilson, born in Devon in 1723, the year that Sir Godfrey Kneller died. As a young man, Reynolds had the opportunity to visit Italy, and it was while he was there that he caught the severe cold that left him permanently deaf. Back in England, in 1753, he set up his studio in Great Newport Street, off St Martin's Lane, later moving to Leicester Fields, where so many artists came to live. He was a kindly, lovable man and after a relatively slow start was soon acknowledged as the master of his profession and was universally popular, not only for his portraiture but for his courtesy and charm. He was knighted a few days before the opening of the Academy, and his life was one of contentment and achievement until 1789, when he lost the sight of one eye, and the sight of the other was threatened. From this calamity he never recovered. As his sight faded, so did his strength, and he died in 1792.

In the piazza, the market continued to flourish and grow.

Boswell records that one night in 1752, when two friends of Dr Johnson, Beauclerk and Langton, had supped at a tavern and sat up till about three in the morning, it came into their heads to go and knock up Johnson and see if they could prevail on him to join them in a ramble. They rapped violently on the door of his chambers in the Temple, till at last he appeared in his shirt, with his little black wig on the top of his head instead of a night-cap, and a poker in his hand, imagining, probably, that some ruffians were coming to attack him. When he discovered who they were, and was told their errand, he smiled and with great good-humour agreed to their proposal.

'He was soon dressed and they sallied forth together into Covent Garden, where the greengrocers and fruiterers were beginning to arrange their hampers, just come in from the country. Johnson made some attempts to help them, but the honest gardeners stared so at his figure and his manner, and odd interference, that he soon saw his services were not relished. They then repaired to one of the neighbouring taverns and made a bowl of that liquor called "Bishop", which Johnson had always liked.'

But it was not until 1763 that the young Boswell first met Johnson and heard all these stories. That famous meeting took place at Tom Davies's bookshop, on the south side of Russell Street, opposite Tom's Coffee House. Boswell was then only twenty-three and wrote: 'On Monday, the 16th of May, when I was sitting in Mr Davies's back parlour, after having drunk tea with him and Mrs Davies, Johnson unexpectedly came into the shop, and Mr Davies having perceived him through the glass door of the room in which we were sitting, advancing towards us ... I found that I had a very perfect idea of Johnson's figure from the portrait of him, painted by Sir Joshua Reynolds, soon after he had published his dictionary, in the attitude of sitting in his easy-chair in deep meditation. Mr Davies mentioned my name and respectfully introduced me.'

It began a friendship which was to last until Johnson's death, twenty-one years later, in 1784; and after that time Boswell said that he never passed Tom Davies's bookshop without feelings of 'reverence and regret'; but ultimately the shop failed and became yet another coffee-house, 'The Caledonien'.

Until the end of the century, the market continued to spread untidily throughout the whole three acres of the square. On the southern side the long, continuous row of single-storeyed shops still stood for a time, but now on the east side were scattered shops and booths. There were more shops in the north-west corner, while in the centre and along the north side was an untidy collection of roofed but open-sided booths and tumbledown sheds, in many of which people lived in varying degrees of squalor. And amongst them were now butchers and bakers and pedlars of illicit gin.

Covent Garden market has become 'an instance of the pernicious effect of neglect and filth on the public taste and morality, in a spot where large numbers of people daily congregate', declared one of the Bow Street magistrates. 'It is surely a great error to spend nearly a million of money on a penitentiary, whilst the hotbeds of vice from which it is filled are wholly unattended to. What must necessarily be the moral state of the numerous class constantly exposed to the changes of weather, amidst the mud and putridities of Covent Garden? What ought it to be where the occupation is amongst vegetables, fruit and flowers, if there were well-regulated accommodations?'

The traffic in Covent Garden had always been a problem. The narrow streets where the threatres stood were congested by the sedan chairs and their bearers in the earlier part of the century and by the long lines of carriages in the later years, while from the early hours of the morning until mid-afternoon the carts and drays of the market people struggled to make their way through, with their cumbersome loads of fruit and vegetables.

As the residents saw the unsightly market buildings spreading and the unwieldy traffic increasing, they at last lodged a complaint with the Duke of Bedford, begging him to 'take the favourable occasion that will soon offer, by the expiration of the lease of the Market, to become the happy instrument of reviving the decayed credit of the parish and restoring it to its pristine flourishing state ... ' However, the Duke did nothing of the kind. He ignored the petition. The market remained and continued to spread, while more residents moved away. As the lovely old houses were deserted, some were taken over by the market people, others by disreputable members of London's underworld, who let them fall into a state of almost irremediable decay; and when, in 1769, the south-eastern part of the Little Piazza was burnt down, it was never rebuilt.

Yet in the surrounding streets, the artists, poets and theatre people were still living, in a state of Bohemian contentment, and for a time Covent Garden became fashionable for its mercers and woollen drapers.

At the beginning of Georgian times, the best shopping districts in London for drapery and all manner of clothing were still in the City

– particularly the Royal Exchange, St Paul's churchyard and Ludgate Hill – but by the middle of the century they had moved westwards.

In 1753 the fourth Duke of Bedford was buying cloth – blue, claret, white and blossom colour – from Gabriel Fouace at the 'Pearl and Crown' in Bedford Street, Covent Garden, at 17 shillings a yard, and also from James Morris at the 'Black Spread Eagle' and 'King's Arms' in Russell Street. One of the most famous mercer's shops was Hinchill and Croft in Henrietta Street, selling brocade to the Duke at 25 shillings a yard, Genoa velvet at 27 shillings and an ordinary silk, called 'tabby', for only 9/6d a yard. Another excellent mercer's was Mason, Lucas and Higgins, at the 'Lamb' in Chandos Street. Gold lace was sold by Peter Bunnell, the laceman, at the 'Golden Cock' in Bedford Street, at 18 shillings a yard, but he gave good value for old lace, which was often used again on new clothes.

In 1741 Mrs Purefoy, mother of Henry Purefoy, Lord of the Manor of Shalstone, near Brackley, was writing to a shop in Covent Garden for 'a very good whale bone hoop petticoat of the newest fashion', which was to be sent by the Buckingham carrier, Mrs Eagles, 'who inns at the GEORGE in Smithfield and leaves London on Tuesday morning about 4 a.m.'.

It was an unsatisfactory way to buy clothes. Henry was always writing to London to ask his tailor for the latest fashion news and for patterns of 'super fine cloth'. 'Do they button their Cloathes with Silver or Gold Buttons or continue to wear laced waistcoats of silk or cloth?' he asks. On another occasion he complains bitterly: 'The Gold laced waistcoat you made mee last year has done you no credit in the making, it gapes so intolerably before at the bottom, when I button it at ye waistbone of my breeches and stand upright it gapes at the bottom beyond my breeches and everybody takes notice of it. As to my size I am partly the same bignesse as I was when in Town last, but you made the last cloathes a little too straight.'

False teeth were a problem, and Mrs Purefoy, with an optimism born perhaps of desperation, sent to Mr Coryndon, 'Operator for ye teeth near the new Church in ye Strand', for a new set of teeth, marking on a piece of wood the places where her own teeth remained and giving the measurement of her gums on a piece of tape. But when they arrived, the poor soul complained that the spaces he had left did not match with her own teeth and the bite was too high on the two 'hind' teeth.

However, fashionable retailing was soon moving still farther west. Although the Duke of Bedford had been buying his hats from William Finch, at the corner of Tavistock Street and Southampton Street, by 1759 he was buying them in St James's Street from Mr James Lock, where a fine beaver hat cost him £1 and six double cockades 9 shillings.

Covent Garden was also, for a time, the centre of the manufacture of the new mahogany furniture. The story goes that 'Dr Gibbons, an eminent physician of the time, was building a house in King Street, when his brother, a West Indian captain, brought over some mahogany as ballast, and thinking the wood might be of service to his brother, the doctor, he sent him a quantity of it; but the carpenters finding it too hard to work, it was laid aside. Soon after this, Mrs Gibbons wanting a candle-box, the doctor called on his cabinet-maker in Long Acre, and asked him to make one of some wood that lay in his garden. He complained, however, that it was too hard for his tools, and the doctor said he must get some stronger tools. The box was made and approved, so that the doctor had a bureau made of the same wood; the fine colour and polish were so pleasing that he invited his friends to come and see the bureau; and amongst them was the Duchess of Buckingham, through whose patronage of it the wood came into general use.' *

At the beginning of Georgian times, solid walnut, or more often walnut veneer on beech or some similar, relatively inexpensive wood, was used for the better kinds of furniture, although solid oak was still used in country districts, but mahogany, or Spanish mahogany as it was then called, was now imported in increasingly large quantities from the West Indies. It was hard, heavy and reliable, and soon became more popular than walnut, so that for many years to come it was used almost exclusively for furniture. Throughout the first half of the century there were no striking developments in design. The cabinet-makers were turning out pieces of impeccable workmanship but very much in the Queen Anne style. The new development came about 1745, when Chippendale, a brilliant master cabinet-maker, opened workshops in Long Acre and then, in 1753, in St Martin's Lane. The following year he published a trade catalogue, *The Gentleman's and Cabinet Maker's Directory*, which contained many furniture designs, some already in use but some that were new, with

* *Annals of Covent Garden*, E. Beresford Chancellor (Hutchinson, 1930)

directions for making them. The furniture from Chippendale's workshops in Covent Garden, and from other cabinet-makers who used his book, became immensely popular, and the Chippendale period had begun.

Hepplewhite appeared a few years later, opening his business in Cripplegate, but Robert Adam, primarily an architect, designed furniture to match the style of decoration of his rooms, passing the designs on to the practical cabinet-makers, and much of this furniture was made for him by the Chippendale workshops, which remained in St Martin's Lane until 1813.

Many of the houses of Covent Garden, particularly in King Street, had mahogany front doors, and in Goodwin's Court, that delightful little row of bow-fronted houses leading from St Martin's Lane, they remain to this day.

From 1768 to 1774 Josiah Wedgwood had his showrooms of pottery and porcelain in a house at the corner of Great Newport Street and St Martin's Lane. He produced pottery and china which every one could afford, and he turned it out, at his family's potteries in Burslem, in such large quantities that it set the universal fashion for chinaware and the decline in the use of pewter. He perfected a white English earthenware and began to experiment. His shapes, colours and designs were excellent, and he used John Flaxman to design the characteristic Wedgwood decoration of classical figures, many of which were copied from the frescoes at Pompeii.

Wedgwood's house in St Martin's Lane is no longer standing, but he described it as 'at the top of St Martin's Lane, a corner house 60 feet long; the streets are wide which lye to it, and carriages may come to it either from Westminster or the City without being incommoded with drays full of timber and coals, which are always pouring in from the various wharfs, and making stops in the Strand very disagreeable and sometimes dangerous ... My friends in town tell me that it is the best situation in London for my rooms.'

It was a double-fronted house, the ground floor being used for the sale of ordinary goods, where 'the public entered in and out at pleasure.' On the first floor was a gallery where Wedgwood's wealthy and aristocratic customers did their business, and the second floor was the family's London home.

The French fashion for papier mâché, particularly for painted trays, began about this time in Covent Garden. In the early days, in order to keep the process a secret, and before a machine was devised for mashing the paper, two old Frenchwomen established themselves in James Street, having come over from France for the express purpose of chewing cuttings of paper all day long, which they bought from the surrounding stationers and book-binders.

When Mrs Nollekens asked a fruiterer in the market if he could tell her the house in James Street where Charles Crignion, the engraver, had once lived, he said at once: 'Number 27. I recollect the old house when it was a shop inhabited by two old French women, who came over here to chew paper for the papier-mâché people.'

The memoirs of William Hickey, a younger contemporary of Boswell, give a picture of another Covent Garden life, which flourished alongside all these wonderful achievements of art, literature, music and the theatre, with the relentlessly growing market in its midst.

He was born in 1749, in St Albans Street, Pall Mall, the son of a prosperous attorney. By the time he was eight, he had been seduced by his sisters' nursemaid, who was summarily dismissed when they were discovered. He was expelled from Westminster school for playing truant. From his next school, at Streatham, he and two friends slipped away one day and, with two girls they had met, went off to Covent Garden to see a new play, after which they had supper at the Shakespeare, with a plentiful supply of punch, and took a hackney back to Westminster, where they picked up their horses. They rode back to Streatham and arrived at the school at a quarter to three in the morning. Hickey was again threatened with expulsion, but he was now seventeen, and his father had in any case decided it was time for him to leave, so he was articled to his father's partner, Mr Bayley.

At this time, he had his hair tied, 'turned over my forehead, powdered, pomatumed, and three curls on either side, with a thick false tail,' he said, 'done by Nerot, a fashionable French hair dresser and peruke maker, judged to be the best in London'.

For eight months his conduct was irreproachable, but then the nursemaid, Nancy Harris, discovered him again, and, as his parents were away at their country house at Twickenham, she took him back to her lodgings in Berwick Street, where he stayed for several nights. His elder brother, also an apprentice with Mr Bayley, discovered where he had been and informed Bayley himself, who called on Nancy and warned her that if she persisted in receiving William, he would have her committed to hard labour in the Bridewell, for

19 Colley Cibber, *c.* 1740

20 Francis Heyman's version of David Garrick and Mrs Pritchard in *The Suspicious Husband c.* 1747/50

21 The 'Screen Scene' from Sheridan's *School for Scandal* at Drury Lane, 1777

22 Reynold's portrait of Dr Johnson, 1756

23 Bow Street Police Court in the time of Sir John Fielding

24 Going home from Tom King's Coffee House

25 The Caledonian, formerly Britton's Coffee House, from a watercolour by T. H. She

26 The burning of Covent Garden Theatre

27 Theatre Royal, Drury Lane in 1776

29 Drury Lane, 1808.
Engraving from an
aquatint by Pugin and
Rowlandson

30 Gainsborough's portrait of Mary Robinson

31 Sarah Siddons by Romney

32 The market in 1812

33 An oil sketch of Edmund
Kean by Clint

34 Charles and Mary Lamb in 1834,
the year of Charles's death

inveigling away and harbouring an apprentice. William then promised never to stay out at night and never again to go to Berwick Street. So Nancy moved to Cecil Street, off the Strand, and William contrived to visit her during the daytime.

'I now became a constant frequenter of the Bedford and Piazza coffee houses,' he records, 'but my chief place for eating was Young Slaughter's in St Martin's Lane, where I supped every night with a set of extravagant young men of my own stamp. After some time we were displeased with the noise, and the promiscuous company that frequented the Coffee room, chiefly to read the newspapers, especially half a dozen respectable old men, who we impertinently pronounced a set of stupid, formal ancient prigs, horrid periwig bores, every way unfit to herd with such bloods as us. It was therefore resolved that we should have private rooms upstairs, where we established ourselves into a roaring club, supped at eleven, after which we usually adjoined to Bow Street, Covent Garden, in which street there were then three most notorious Bawdy houses, all of which we took in rotation ... The third brothel was kept by Mother Cocksedge ... and it will scarcely be credited that the house was actually next, of course under the very nose of that vigilant and upright magistrate, Sir John Fielding, who, from the riotous proceedings I have been witness to at his worthy neighbour's, must have been deaf as well as blind, or at least, well paid for affecting to be so.

'In these houses we usually spent three to four hours, drinking Arrack punch ... and romping and playing all sorts of tricks with the girls. At a late date, or rather early hour in the morning, we separated, retiring to the private lodgings of some of the girls, there being only two that resided in the house, or our homes, as fancy led, or according to the state of our finances.'

The Bedford Coffee House, where Hickey made his trip from Streatham, had been converted from Sir Edmund Verney's house at the east end of the piazza, next to Russell Street, and was a popular resort of writers, artists and theatre people throughout the eighteenth century. Here Foote held forth at his own corner table, as Dryden had done at Will's and Addison at Button's. Fielding, Goldsmith, Hogarth and Churchill all met here, and later it was the resort of Quin, David Garrick, Arthur Murphy, Macklin and Sheridan.

The Connoisseur of 31 January 1754 described the Bedford as being nightly crowded with men of parts. 'Almost every one you meet is a polite scholar and wit. Jokes and bon-mots are echoed from box to box. Every branch of literature is critically examined, and the merit of every production of the press, or performance of the theatres, weighed and determined.'

The Piazza Coffee House was on the site of the Tavistock Hotel, and the Shakespeare Tavern, one of the earliest to be built in Covent Garden, adjoined it.

In St Martin's Lane there were two 'Slaughter's'. 'Old Slaughter's', established by Thomas Slaughter in 1692, was on the west side, a few doors from Newport Street. It was the favourite meeting-place of artists, notably Hogarth and later David Wilks and Benjamin Haydon. It was called 'Old Slaughter's' when, in the 1720s, another coffee-house, 'Young Slaughter's', was established only a few doors away, and this became the haunt of men of science – and the home of a club which included John Hunter, Captain Cook and Sir Joseph Banks. The old places were demolished when Cranbourn Street was formed, in 1842.

Hickey and his circle were probably completely unaware of the quality of the men they saw at these places, but Hickey himself quietened down for a few months, after a friend of the family had committed suicide, after incurring a gambling debt of £10,000, in one night's play at White's, in St James's Street.

Then he decided to visit his old friends at Slaughter's again. They greeted him warmly and decided to celebrate his return. 'Up I went to the Club room, down went the wine and punch, and away went all my plans of reformation,' said William.

They sallied forth and went the old Bow Street rounds, and then he was led into 'an absolute hell on earth. The first impression on my mind upon entering those diabolical regions never will be effaced from my memory. The den was distinguished by the name of Wetherby's, situate in the narrowest part of Little Russell Street, Drury Lane.* Upon ringing at a door, strongly secured with knobs of iron, a cut-throat looking rascal opened a small wicket, which was also secured with narrow iron bars, who in a hoarse and ferocious voice asked "Who's there?" Being answered "Friends," we were cautiously admitted one at a time, and when the last had entered, the door was instantly closed and secured, not only by an immense lock and key, but a massive iron bolt and chain.'

* Until 1859, Russell Street was known as Great Russell Street from Bow Street to the market and Little Russell Street from Bow Street to Drury Lane.

When they reached the main room, it was in an uproar: ' ... men and women promiscuously mounted upon chairs, tables and benches, in order to see a sort of general conflict carried on upon the floor. Two she-devils, for they scarce had a human appearance, were engaged in a scratching and boxing match, their faces entirely covered with blood, bosoms bare, and the clothes nearly torn from their bodies. For several minutes not a creature interfered between them or seemed to care a straw what mischief they might do each other, and the contest went on with unabated fury.

'In another corner of the same room, an uncommonly athletic young man of about twenty-five seemed to be the object of universal attack. No less than three Amazonian tigresses were pummelling him with all their might, and it appeared to me that some of the males at times dealt him blows with their sticks.'

After an hour or two 'in this dreadful hole', his friends dragged him to 'another scene of nocturnal dissoluteness, situate in the same street, but on the opposite side. This was called Murphy's. From this latter nest of pickpockets, and lowest description of prostitutes we got away about half past four, I inwardly wishing every mishap might attend me if ever I again crossed the threshold of either of the Russell Street houses during the remainder of my life.'

He continued frequenting the club at Slaughter's, however, and also dined regularly at the Shakespeare, and his friends, telling him that the visit to Wetherby's had been on an unfortunate evening, persuaded him to go there again. He now met one of the ferocious fighting women, whose name was Burgess, and she told him that she and her combatant had been unusually drunk on his previous visit and had quarrelled in their cups. As for the other fight, the man, 'who was a notorious woman bully', had basely robbed the two who had attacked him. On this visit Miss Burgess 'sang a number of admirable songs, and was very entertaining, as was another sad profligate girl, who had justly acquired the name of Blasted Bet Wilkinson'.

William made further good resolutions but met trouble again after a chance encounter with two friends who invited him to a party at the Shakespeare, at which there were seven or eight men and women, all 'hard-goers'. The master of the house warned Hickey that he was in bad company, but he took no notice and drank and drank until he was 'past all recollection'.

He woke up in 'a strange, dismal-looking room, his head aching horribly, pains of a violent nature in every limb and deadly sickness at the stomach'. He got out of bed and looked out of the window but could see nothing but the backs of old houses, 'from which various emblems of poverty were displayed, such as ragged shifts, petticoats and other parts of female wardrobes hanging to dry'. He then found that his pockets were empty and that his gold watch and other jewellery and all his money had gone. He rang a bell three or four times, and at last a man appeared, who told him that he was in the Cross Keys Bagnio in Little Russell Street, having been brought there by the watchman at five o'clock in the morning, in 'woeful plight'.

He had been turned out of Wetherby's, and they had been about to carry him to the Covent Garden watch-house, to await the magistrate, but two of the watchmen and a waiter had pleaded for him, for he had often given them a shilling for drinks, and they had taken him to the bagnio instead. The watchman had saved his watch for him, but said his pockets were already empty when they found him.

Hickey had two other Covent Garden haunts 'of the same stamp, or if the degree of depravity and infamy would admit, even worse. The one was facetiously called "The Soup Shop", a dirty, vile ale house in Bridge Street, Drury Lane; the other was significantly named "The Finish". This was a shed in Covent Garden market, once dignified by the title of "Carpenter's Coffee House".'

This was originally called the 'King's Head'. It was on the south side of the square, kept by Mrs Butler, and here footpads and highwaymen mixed with the young bloods. It kept open all night and was the last of the night taverns in Covent Garden, not being cleared away until 1829.

Tom King's coffee-house was in front of the church. Tom was well born but had run away from Eton and married the notorious Moll; after his early death, Moll King had run the place on her own, entertaining the rakes of the town all through the night and providing them with prostitutes. 'The eminent, the eccentric, and the notorious in every walk of life were to be found nightly indulging their festivities within its famous precincts ... Moll King would serve chimney-sweeps, gardeners and the market people in common with her lords of the highest rank.'

At last the place became so disreputable and scandalous that, in 1739, Moll was arrested, charged with keeping a disorderly house and committed to the King's Bench prison. By the time she was released, the coffee-house had been pulled down, and Moll retired to Hampstead and respectability, became a regular church-goer and lived in peace and propriety until she died in 1747.

Betty Careless was a few years before Hickey's time, but she was another highly successful prostitute, although she fell on hard times in the end and died penniless. Yet she achieved an obituary notice in the *Gentleman's Magazine*, which in April 1752 announced: 'Was buried from the Poor-house of St Paul's, Covent Garden, the famed Betty Careless, who had helped the gay gentlemen of this country to squander £50,000.'

It was in 1749, the year that Hickey was born, that John Cleland published his *Fanny Hill*, and the original of his Mrs Cole was almost certainly Mother Douglas, nicknamed Coals, whose house was in the piazza. Like William Hickey, Cleland, born forty years earlier, had been educated at Westminster school, and then he joined the East India Company, but he never stayed anywhere for long, and when he eventually arrived back in England, he had hardly any money and was from time to time imprisoned for debt. He wrote *Fanny Hill – The Memoirs of a Woman of Pleasure* to avoid another spell of imprisonment, and sold it to a publisher in St Paul's churchyard for £25. It is a beautifully written piece of erotica, which shocked the Church and was banned for the next two centuries or more, but not before the publishers had made a small fortune from it, estimated at some £10,000. It gives a vivid picture of the life of a Covent Garden prostitute during the years when Hickey was growing up.

Fanny was an innocent country girl from a village in Lancashire. She was barely fifteen when both her parents died of smallpox, and she was left friendless and almost penniless, with just enough money to make her way to London, 'to seek her fortune'. She made her way to an 'intelligence office' to look for work. Mrs Brown had also called at the office that morning, looking for likely girls for her brothel. Fanny was very pretty, and when Mrs Brown offered her work 'as her servant and friend', she gladly accepted, having no idea what else was involved. Her career was soon under way, but within a few weeks she fell in love with one of her clients, a handsome young man called Charles. She ran away from Mrs Brown, and he set her up in rooms in St James's, where for a while they were blissfully happy. But suddenly Charles disappeared. Fanny soon learnt that his father had packed him off to the South Seas at such short notice that he had

had no chance to tell her what had happened.

Fanny was nearly penniless again and, after many adventures, ended up with Mrs Cole, whose house in the piazza was discreetly disguised as a milliner's shop. Three of her girls spent most of their time there, making hats, but the rest of the girls, as at the brothels which Hickey visited, lived close by, in their own lodgings.

Fanny's story ended happily, for one of the elderly clients left her a fortune, and then Charles turned up again, still in love with her: and Cleland saw to it that they were married and lived happily ever after.

Hickey in his *Memoirs* wrote about the four profligate young men who formed the original band of Mohawks. These wild young men first came to notice in the winter of 1771, and 'from the profligacy of their manners and their outrageous conduct in the theatres, taverns and coffee houses in the vicinity of Covent Garden, created general indignation and alarm, actually driving away many sedate persons from their customary arrangements in an evening. They were severely attacked in the newspapers but this only seemed to stimulate their excesses! Their leader was a wealthy young man, Rhoan Hamilton, the second in command was Hayter, son of a rich merchant and bank director, the third was Osborne, a young American who had come to England to study law, and the fourth was Mr Frederick, handsome but penniless, the grandson of the unfortunate Theodore, King of Corsica, the Prussian soldier of fortune who, while serving with Charles XII of Sweden, was invited by the simple, impoverished people of Corsica to become their King, in return for his protection. But he was alleged to have coined money from them and had to flee for his life, eventually arriving penniless in London, where he soon landed in a debtors' prison.

These four young men, nearly always drunk, sometimes acted separately but met every evening at the same time, to plan their mischief for the following day. They had a run of three years, 'In an uninterrupted course of folly, intemperance and riot, to the utter disgrace of themselves, and of the police of the capital, which was either so relaxed, or so corrupt as to permit their course of iniquity to proceed uninterrupted ...'. Early in 1774, however, after deliberately creating a riot at the Covent Garden theatre, where they began insulting and fighting some of the audience, they were carried off bodily to the watch-house, and in the morning the justices of Bow Street remanded them on bail for very large amounts. Hamilton forfeited his bail and, after paying some of his tradesmen's bills, fled to Paris. Hayter's father sent him to Holland. Osborne, no longer able to borrow from Hamilton, found himself bankrupt and returned to America, taking Frederick with him. Frederick enlisted in one of the English regiments over there and did well, obtaining a commission, but he was killed soon afterwards, during the American War of Independence.

Hickey himself at last settled down to become a respectable lawyer and ended his *Memoirs* by saying: 'My only consolation is that although my follies (not to use a harsher term) were so numerous and so often repeated, yet my honoured father lived long enough to see an end to them, and most heartily and affectionately to congratulate me upon my having at last steadily settled in a fair, industrious, and honourable line of life, universally esteemed and respected in the society amongst whom I resided.'

7

Leading Ladies

In 1763 Garrick, feeling tired and not in the best of health, left the stage for a time and went abroad with his wife for a year or two, William Powell taking his place at the theatre. But when, two years later, he was back in London, the young George III told him he must not retire and brought him back to the stage of Drury Lane with a command performance of *Much Ado About Nothing*. He was more popular than ever, and everyone was anxious to see him. 'When Garrick acted,' said Mrs Carter, the Bluestocking whom Dr Johnson so much admired, 'hackney chairs were then so numerous that they stood all round the Piazzas, down Southampton Street, and extended more than halfway along Maiden Lane.'

Lacy died in 1774, leaving his son Willoughby to succeed him, but Garrick did not trust his judgement, and he was also having trouble with his leading ladies. Miss Pope, the comedienne, he told to leave; Miss Younge and Mrs Yates he considered affected and pretentious; while Mrs Abington, the original Lady Teazle, he detested. She was a cobbler's daughter who had begun life as a flower-girl but rose in the world to give elaborate supper parties to the smartest of London society. Garrick said she was a jealous, conceited, nagging woman, 'below the thought of any honest man or woman ... as silly as she is false and treacherous'. And at fifty-eight she was getting far too old for youthful parts and was tending to forget her lines. So in 1776 she retired.

In 1772, thirteen years before the advent of *The Times*, Covent Garden saw the birth of a new English newspaper, the *Morning Post*, which was established in Wellington Street and was to last until 1937, when it was merged with the *Daily Telegraph*. It was a good time for journalists for they were at last given a measure of freedom to report Parliamentary proceedings; at the same time the improvement of the daily posts between London and the Home Counties meant that the London Press was having a far wider circulation. But these early newspapers relied to a great extent on revenue from advertising, and its first title was *The Morning Post and Daily Advertising Pamphlet*. Thus, in the first numbers, besides advertisements for books and Christie's auction rooms, money-lenders for mortgages and annuities, linen drapers, houses for sale and to let, servants looking for work and households looking for servants, a 'Most Efficacious Remedy for Scurvy and Rheumatism' and 'Ointment for the Itch', were announcements that the Theatre Royal in Drury Lane would be presenting *The Maid of the Mill*, Isaac Bickerstaffe's adaptation of Richardson's *Pamela*, and Garrick's *Miss in her Teens*, and the Theatre Royal in Covent Garden, *Henry the Eighth*.

The first editor was the Reverend Henry Bate, who a few years later, on inheriting some property, added the name of Dudley and eventually became Sir Henry Bate Dudley. In the first few years of his editorship he dismissed George Corrall, who promptly, with the help of the printer Edward Cox, set about bringing out a new *Morning Post* which was a blatant copy of the first and promoted a legal battle, which Corrall and Cox lost. They never forgave Henry Bate. They changed the name of their paper to the *New Morning Post* and began a campaign of slander against the older paper and some of their former employers, two of whom they described as 'reverend parsonical banditti who, with all the chicane of sacerdotal hypocrisy, had not only insidiously wormed themselves into the knowledge of the customary emoluments of printing and publishing in general, but have unlawfully possessed themselves of the means of acquiring these emoluments, by particular acts of violence, imposition and rapine perpetrated upon the person of the original Printer and Publisher'. And the proprietors, they said, were 'parasites of the printing industry'.

The *Morning Post* replied with a procession of drums and trumpets, with streamers flying. 'It was a procession set forth by Mr Bate, Lord Lyttelton's chaplain, and author of the old Morning Post, and meant as an appeal to the town against his antagonist, the new one,' wrote Horace Walpole. 'The New Morning Post, I am told, for I never take in either, exceeds all the outrageous Billingsgate that ever was heard of. What a country! ... a solemn and expensive masquerade exhibition by a clergyman in defence of daily scandal against women of the first rank.'

Henry Bate had introduced Mrs Siddons to Garrick that year, as a young and promising actress. She had been born a Kemble, and her family were living in a cottage built in the garden behind 43 King Street. Garrick gave her the part of Portia for her first appearance at Drury Lane, but she was very young and inexperienced and not as successful as he had hoped. However, when Henry Bate offered him his own play, *The Blackamoor Washed White*, which he accepted, he gave Mrs Siddons the lead. Corrall and Cox heard about this and made their plans, but Bate, learning that they were planning mischief, made arrangements of his own, planting professional pugilists in the theatre amongst the audience. The play began – and then came the boos and catcalls. The ladies were asked to leave the theatre. Then pandemonium broke out, and the evening ended in a free-for-all. That first night was the end of the run, and also of Mrs Siddons' appearance that season. She left London to play in the provinces for a few years.

Very soon after this, Mary Darby came to London, and her story, so much of it connected with Covent Garden, is a lesson in the social history of the late eighteenth century. She was born in Bristol in 1758, the daughter of a prosperous merchant in the West Indian trade, and when she was only seven years old she was sent as a weekly boarder to the school run by Hannah More's three sisters, where she found her first love of the theatre, during school visits to the Bristol Theatre Royal.

Then her father, foreseeing that before long Liverpool was to capture a good deal of the Bristol trade, decided to go to America, to investigate the possibilities of whale fishing with the Eskimos of Labrador. Gradually his letters home grew shorter, colder and more infrequent. Then the family solicitor broke the news to Mrs Darby that her husband had lost most of his money in the Labrador venture and to pay his debts had given a bill of sale on the Bristol home and all its contents. Mary, her small brother and her mother were reduced to penury. Mary had to leave school, and for a time they lived in two miserable attics in the poorest part of the city. Then came a letter from Darby, telling them to come to London. His fortunes had revived and he had arranged for Mary to go to a small boarding school, run by Mrs Lorrington in Chelsea, and for Mrs Darby and George to lodge at the nearby vicarage, where the Vicar could teach George; whereupon he returned to America, to live with his mistress, whom he now preferred to his wife.

Mrs Lorrington, with whom Mary had to share a bed, was an alcoholic, having taken to drink to drown her sorrows, after the death of her husband. She was hopelessly in debt, the six boarders were sent home and she was turned out of her house, to become a vagrant, dying a year or so later in the Chelsea workhouse.

Mary was sent to a school in Battersea, where she was happy, but soon the money from America stopped and she had to leave. Mrs Darby now decided to rent a house and run a school of her own in Chelsea. It was successful for a time, but then Robinson turned up again, upbraided his wife for disgracing his name by letting the world know she was a schoolmistress because he was not paying her an adequate allowance, hit her soundly and cancelled the lease of the house, which he had the legal right to do. He installed the family in lodgings in Marylebone, put Mary to school nearby, at Oxford House, and departed once more for America, his last words to Mrs Darby being: 'Take care that no dishonour befalls my daughter. If she's not safe at my return, I'll annihilate you.'

Mary had grown into a lovely girl, with an exceptionally beautiful speaking voice. Her new headmistress sized up her situation, for once again the money had not arrived for her school fees, and, knowing that she would soon have to earn a living, discussed her future with the school dancing-master, who was also the ballet master at the Covent Garden theatre. He took her to an audition at the theatre, and the assistant manager, seeing her promise, agreed to coach her.

Mary was blissfully happy, her mother increasingly worried. In her view, and that of all her friends and family, the stage was not a respectable occupation, and she knew that when Darby came to hear what was happening, he would do something outrageous. However, Mary prevailed, and with the help of their London solicitor, they moved to the house of an elderly widower, Mr Cox, living in Chancery Lane, in order to be near the theatre.

Cox was a theatre-lover himself and a friend of Garrick's. He recognized Mary's gifts and he took her to see him. By this time Garrick was nearly sixty, and his health was failing, particularly since he and Eva had moved at last from their comfortable home in Southampton Street to the new house in the Adelphi Terrace, for grand as it was, it was too close to the river and too often shrouded in the damp, bleak mists which, all through the winter months, crept up from the waterfront.

Garrick spoke Romeo's part to Mary's Juliet, and Lear to her Cordelia. He was delighted with her and said that her voice reminded him of Mrs Cibber's – which had been one of the most beautiful he had ever known. He agreed to continue the coaching which Mr Hull of Covent Garden had begun so effectively and arranged for her to visit Drury Lane as often as she liked, saying that in a few months' time he felt she would be ready to make her professional appearance, and he would like her to play Cordelia to his King Lear.

Mary was in a transport of delight, her mother more worried than ever. The only solution, she felt, was to find a husband for her as quickly as possible, for although Mr Garrick was a gentleman, mixing freely with the best society in the country, she knew that no decent man, of her choosing, would ever consider allowing his wife to be an actress.

During the next few weeks, Mary and her mother were at the theatre most nights, and Mary's exceptional beauty soon caught the eyes of several young men. One in particular was increasingly attentive, and although Mary was not remotely interested in him, Mrs Darby's hopes rose. At last came the day when he had asked to call and make his proposal, but just in time a friend of his arrived to warn Mrs Darby that the young lover was married and had already seduced two or three young girls by the same trick. Disaster was averted, but soon after this poor Mary developed smallpox and was very ill.

Her mother and a new admirer, Thomas Robinson, were both lovingly attentive, but at the same time they began a gentle but persistent persuasion for Mary to give up all thoughts of the stage and marry Tom. At first, ill as she was, she resisted them. Then her mother reminded her that she might be scarred for life with her pockmarks and her beauty ruined. Moreover, they all knew that Mr Garrick would soon be retiring. How did they know that his successor would feel so enthusiastic as Mr Garrick about her abilities?

Mary was weak and ill and in the depths of depression that she might lose her looks. In the end, through Mrs Darby's careful nursing, they found that her face was unblemished. Again she tried to avoid the marriage, but in the end Tom and her mother prevailed, Tom pleasing Mrs Darby by insisting that no wife of his should ever appear on the stage. At the last minute, however, Tom urged that the wedding be kept secret until he had told his uncle, who was to leave him his fortune.

A letter of explanation was sent to Garrick, and the wedding took place. Tom established Mary and Mrs Darby in a beautiful old Inigo Jones house, where Chippendale later came to live, which he rented from the widow of Mr Worlidge, the engraver, at the corner of Great Queen Street and Drury Lane, while he remained for a time at the lodgings of the solicitor in Chancery Lane, to whom he had been articled.

They soon learned that Tom was the illegitimate son of the 'uncle' who was said to be leaving him his fortune, and that, although he was supposed to have completed his articles, being very lazy and staying away from work whenever he felt inclined, he had done no such thing. Tom apologized, promised to work harder and treated Mary well for the next few months, and Mrs Darby returned to Bristol. One night Tom took Mary to the newly opened Pantheon in Oxford Street, and here they met the wicked Lord Lyttelton, who was at once attracted to Mary. He failed to seduce her but succeeded with Tom, whom he egged on to lead the gay life until he was hopelessly in debt. Mary was pregnant and at last, just after the baby was born, Tom was taken to the sheriff's office in Bow Street and told he would be committed to the King's Bench prison until his debts were paid. And Mary, with no home or money, had no choice but to go with him, with the baby.

It was not for another nine months, in the autumn of 1776, that, through the labours of John Howard and the Act for the Relief of Insolvent Debtors, they were set free. Mary was seventeen. She found lodgings for them all in Bond Street, above the shop of Mr Lyne, the confectioner, and tried to earn some money by writing poetry, but she had little success. 'Writing is a destructive pursuit', she confided to her diary.

A few days later, while walking in Hyde Park, she ran into William Brereton, the Drury Lane actor whom she had met three years earlier. He learnt what had happened to her and persuaded her to try again for the stage. Tom, with only his father's allowance of £2 a week, no work and little inclination to find any, now thought the idea was a good one.

In the meantime, Sheridan had arrived at Drury Lane from his home in Bath. He was only twenty-two when, in 1773, he had married the beautiful Elizabeth Linley, and they had come to London, Sheridan spending far more money on the gay life than he could afford. His first play *The Rivals* was presented at Covent Garden in 1775, and although it was not at first a success, with a good deal of revision, it was recognized as a brilliant comedy.

He wrote two or three more plays for Covent Garden and the following year, with the help of his father-in-law Linley and another friend, bought half the patent of Drury Lane from Garrick for £35,000, buying the remainder on mortgage, for £45,000, the following year.

Brereton arranged for Mary to meet Sheridan, and he was so impressed with her that he offered her a salary of £10 a week. The ailing Garrick, who still took an active interest in the theatre, did some final coaching, and on 10 December 1776, a week or two after her eighteenth birthday, Mary made her first appearance on the stage, as Juliet.

With the final curtain, the applause was tumultuous, and more triumphs were to follow during that winter season.

She moved to Southampton Street, to be nearer the theatre, and Tom came with her, accepting the legal right to share her income and her home.

As Juliet, Mary had worn a pale pink satin dress, spangled with silver, and a white feather head-dress, while Brereton, her Romeo, wore the regulation powdered wig, lace-trimmed shirt, velvet coat and breeches, for Garrick still maintained that the public preferred the contemporary dress to authentic, historical costume. However, when Mary played the part of Statira, in Nathaniel Lee's play *Alexander the Great*, she insisted on discarding the fashionable hoop, which nearly every woman in England was wearing at the time, both on and off the stage, and chose instead a draped, classical dress and sandals, which she said made her feel and act more like Statira, and which the audience, notwithstanding Garrick's doubts, readily accepted.

As Mary's success continued, Tom became increasingly intractable, now keeping two mistresses, both living in the same house in Maiden Lane, one a dancer at the Covent Garden theatre, the other a professional prostitute. Although, like Sheridan, he had been to school at Harrow, their lives in Covent Garden could not have been more different. Tom spent his days in the gambling-houses and taverns, with a disreputable crowd of hangers-on, while at Sheridan's green-room parties Mary met many members of London society, including Charles James Fox, who became a very good friend to her, as well as Sir Joshua Reynolds and Dr Johnson.

She heard that a house in the piazza had fallen vacant, in the north-east corner, near the Hummums, and she decided to lease it, for she had always wanted to live in the square itself, and it was nearer than ever to the theatres. The new house was large and elegant, and here Mary spent some of the gayest months of her life. She had developed a passion for cards, and at late-night parties after the theatre her friends joined her to play quadrille and faro. Tom had moved in with her, and after a few weeks he found himself a considerable winner, but most of the money he spent on renting a room close by, where he could drink and entertain his own particular cronies in privacy.

Mary's success that winter was brilliant. She took the lead in plays by Vanbrugh, Dryden and Shakespeare, and her small daughter, Maria, now nearly four years old, was growing into a happy little companion.

The Garricks were in London that autumn of 1778, the year that Sheridan's *School for Scandal* first appeared, and spent Christmas as usual with their old friends the Spencers, at Althorp. But here Garrick fell ill again, with what seemed to be nothing worse than a heavy cold and his old enemy, gout. He was driven back from Althorp to the Adelphi in easy stages and for a day or two seemed to be getting better, but then he had a relapse, and on 20 January 1779 he suddenly collapsed and died. He was only sixty-one and was deeply mourned by a host of friends and admirers; at his funeral at Westminster Abbey the procession of mourners, protected by mounted guardsmen, took up all the space between the Adelphi and the Abbey. It began to move at one o'clock, and it was not until three o'clock that the coffin was received at the West Door by the Dean.

Mrs Garrick survived him for more than thirty years, dying in 1822, at the age of ninety-nine, 'a little bowed-down old woman who went about leaning on a gold-headed cane, dressed in deep widow's mourning, and always talking of her dear Davy'.

Dr Johnson, whose own days were now drawing towards the end, said of him that, 'his profession made him rich, and he made his profession respectable.'

Garrick was a fascinating man, elegant, graceful and sweet-natured. He was said to have been vain, sometimes jealous and sometimes querulous, but he was incapable of sustaining any animosity for long, and although he had a reputation for meanness in some matters, he was fundamentally exceedingly generous. As a dramatist he was not in the first rank, most of his plays being adaptations of other people's work, but as an actor he was unsurpassed.

It was at the end of that year of his death, 1779, that Sheridan received a notice that George III had commanded a special performance at Drury Lane for 3 December. He chose *A Winter's Tale*, and Mary was cast as Perdita. The young Prince of Wales was present, and that night he fell madly in love with Mary. Through his friend Lord Malden he sent messages begging her to meet him. He wrote her passionate, imploring letters, to all of which she replied tactfully and evasively. Day after day he wrote, and at last, after six months, she agreed to a secret meeting, arranged by Lord Malden, in the garden of Kew Palace. They met several times after that, the Prince growing more passionately in love with her as the weeks passed. Then, enclosed with a letter in which he begged her to leave the stage, so that they could see more of each other, he enclosed a promissory note for £20,000, sealed with the royal arms, stating that it was to be paid to her when he came of age, for he was still only seventeen.

Mary's marriage had collapsed beyond any hope of redemption. Coming home from the theatre earlier than usual one day, she had found Tom in her bedroom, making love to her maid. She was tired and overwrought and had fallen in love with the handsome young Prince. She yielded at last and, despite Sheridan's warning and advice, resigned from the theatre at the end of that winter season of 1780, left the house in the piazza and, in her own name, took a house in Cork Street, which she furnished luxuriously. On his eighteenth birthday, the Prince was given his own suite of rooms at Buckingham Palace and a certain measure of freedom. He was able to see Mary often, and for the next two years she was his mistress. They lived in the grand manner, wildly extravagant and seen everywhere, both of them beautifully dressed, and 'Perdita', as the Prince always called her, riding in a magnificent coach which had cost the Prince 900 guineas. They were both running into debt, but they were young and in love, and the Prince, after all, was heir to the throne and when he came of age would be given a larger allowance.

Although the serious newspapers were well-established by now, the Grub Street hacks, who had done service in the earlier years, relying for their news mainly on hearsay and backstairs confidences, were still at work, and they gossiped and lampooned the love affair of the Prince of Wales mercilessly. Mary began to receive scurrilous, anonymous letters. She was mobbed and jeered when she appeared alone in her coach or went shopping. Yet she was so happy that she cheerfully ignored it all, for the Prince's devotion made it of little account.

They were seen together in Hyde Park, at Richmond, at parties and receptions. The Duke of Cumberland, whom the Prince had hardly known until now, since neither the Duke nor his wife was received at Court, invited them to card parties at Cumberland House in Pall Mall, although this was probably more to annoy his brother, King George III, than to gratify his nephew, for the King and Queen could not have failed to know about the affair by now, although as yet they had chosen to ignore it.

When the Prince was nineteen, he was allowed his own establishment at Carlton House, and in addition to his receiving an income of £63,000 a year, his debts, amounting to £30,000, were paid. Their money troubles seemed to be over, but just as the Prince was preparing to move into Carlton House there came, without any warning, the fatal note for 'Perdita' – 'We must meet no more.'

The reason for his change of heart seems to have been no more than an encounter with another young woman whom he decided he preferred, and Mary was left with debts of £7,000 and a capital of less than £70, for the Prince had kept none of his promises to pay the expenses of the house in Cork Street, and the promissory note for £20,000 he had sent her, having been made before he was of age, was not valid.

Charles James Fox and Malden did what they could to help her. Fox asked Sheridan to take her back at Drury Lane, but Sheridan regretfully said that the affair had been so publicized in the scandal sheets that he dare not. She would be booed off the stage, and the livelihood of the rest of the cast put in jeopardy.

Sheridan was now a very busy man. In 1780, the year that 'Perdita' had left Covent Garden, he had been elected member for Stafford, and now he had just become Under-Secretary for Foreign Affairs under Rockingham; he was soon to become Secretary to the Treasury in the Coalition Government of 1783.

Malden approached Colonel Hotham, a member of the Prince's household, who agreed that 'Perdita' should be paid £5,000 if she sent back all the Prince's letters. This she did, and by selling nearly all her possessions, including her horse and the beautiful carriage, she managed to satisfy her debtors, but not until 1785 did Fox persuade the Prince to make a legal settlement on her, as a recompense for the havoc he had wrought in her life. This was £500 a year, with £250 a year for Maria after Mary's death.

Mrs Darby was in difficulties once more, for Darby was again in financial trouble in America, so Mary took rooms in Berkeley Square for her, as well as herself and Maria, who was now six years old. Fox introduced her to his young friend Colonel Banastre Tarleton, just back from active service in the American War of Independence. He was the same age as Mary, and he was enchanted by her, for she was still only twenty-six and very beautiful. She helped him write his *History of the British Campaign in the Southern States*, and although she stayed away from the theatres, he gave her all the news from Drury Lane.

Sheridan had introduced the lovable little clown Grimaldi into his Christmas pantomime, and he was proving a great success, soon becoming an institution and a constant source of delight. Robert Baddeley was now one of Sheridan's outstanding players and was to be the last of the Drury Lane players to wear the royal livery off-stage.

Mrs Sarah Siddons had returned to Drury Lane in 1782 and this time was an unqualified success, proving herself to be one of the most compelling tragediennes the theatre had ever known. The whole of fashionable London came to see her. She was an individualist, as Garrick had been, and despite Sheridan's protests, she insisted on deviating from Mrs Pritchard's long-established interpretation of Lady Macbeth in the sleep-walking scene. Mrs Siddons set down her candle and wrung her hands in true anguish, so painful that James Sheridan Knowles, playing opposite her, declared afterwards: 'I smelt blood! I swear I smelt blood!'

She was an extremely beautiful woman, but so great were her powers of empathy that she could make herself look utterly worn and emaciated, where the part called for it. Her eyes would become lustreless and not only her voice but her whole body seemed to undergo a physical change; and the spell-bound audience was often moved to tears by her pathos.

She introduced her brother, John Kemble, to the Lane. Although he did not possess his sister's genius, he was a tall, impressive figure, and his acting was dignified and restrained. His style was different from Garrick's – more classical and less naturalistic – but he brought intelligence and sympathy to his interpretations, and he soon became Sheridan's leading man and manager.

All this poor 'Perdita' must have heard with bitter regrets for her own lost career.

There had been other excitements in Covent Garden. The eastern portico of the church was, for many years, used as the hustings for the Westminster elections. Before the Reform Bill of 1832, these elections were full-blooded, riotous affairs, and none more so than those of 1784, when Sir Cecil Wray and his Tory supporters were making a desperate effort against Charles James Fox. The elections lasted for more than a fortnight, and as the days passed and the voting kept almost even, the partisans threw themselves with ever more zeal into the business of seeking out the more reluctant electors and urging them to come and register their votes. The Duchess of Devonshire took lodgings in Henrietta Street, to be at the scene of operations, and she and her sister, Lady Duncannon, both staunch Whigs, worked with furious fervour for Fox.

'These ladies being furnished with lists of outlying voters, drove in their carriages to their respective dwellings, sparing neither entreaties nor promises. In some instances even personal caresses were said to have been permitted in order to prevail on the sulky and inflexible,' wrote N.W. Wraxhall, 'and there can be no doubt of common mechanics having been conveyed to the hustings by the Duchess in her own coach.'

They said she was offering a kiss for a vote. Fox drew ahead. The Countess of Salisbury began counter-operations on behalf of Wray, but she was too late. Fox, returned with a majority of 235, was victoriously cheered through the streets from Covent Garden to Carlton House, for at this time the Prince of Wales was courting the Whigs.

'All minor interests were swallowed up in this struggle,' wrote an observer, 'which held not only the capital, but also the nation, in suspense, while it rendered Covent Garden and its neighbourhood, during three successive weeks, a scene of outrage and even blood.' Others wrote that 'the vulgar abuse of the candidates from the vilest rabble is not rendered endurable by either wit or good temper.' The indefatigable Duchess of Devonshire, at work by eight o'clock in the morning, canvassed in 'the most blackguard houses in Long Acre'.

This was the year that Dr Johnson died. Very soon afterwards,

Boswell, still drinking as hard as ever, settled down in his house in Great Queen Street, only a few yards from where 'Perdita' had once lived, to begin his life of the great man. It took him several years, being first published in 1791, only four years before he himself died.

Sheridan's wife Elizabeth died, and three years later he married a daughter of the Dean of Winchester.

'Perdita' was very ill by this time. She had gone to Paris for a time, after the break with the Prince, where she was received at the Court of Marie Antoinette and pursued, though in vain, by the Duc d'Orléans. While there she had a letter from Tarleton saying that he was being pressed by his creditors for £150 and must leave the country or be arrested for debt. Mary had just about enough money to help him, and made a dash back to London, but when she reached his lodgings, the landlady said he had already left for Newhaven. Mary persuaded a coachman to drive her down there forthwith and caught Tarleton just as he was about to board a barque laden with contraband for the French coast. But she arrived drenched to the skin, for it had been raining for hours and the coach was old and the windows broken. By the time they were back in London, she had developed rheumatic fever and was desperately ill for weeks; when she was at last able to leave her bed, she was left with rheumatoid arthritis, which became increasingly crippling.

She began to write poems and essays for the newspapers, and had a small measure of success. Then Fox promised to introduce her to the editor of the *Morning Post*, John Taylor, but before he had time to do so, Taylor had resigned, for the paper was doing badly at this time, with a circulation of only 350 copies a day, its supporters having deserted it for the recently established *Times*.

Tarleton who, for so many years, remorseful that her illness had come about through helping him, had been her faithful friend, now wrote to tell her that he was marrying the daughter of the Duke of Ancaster and that they were shortly leaving on a government mission to Portugal. Mary had no one to turn to and was badly in need of money.

Then she read that the *Morning Post* and its offices, now in Catherine Street, had been bought by Daniel Stuart, for £600. She sent him an elegy she had written on the death of Marie Antoinette, and he wrote back saying that he liked it and would publish it for half a guinea. She sent him more poems and they were all accepted, for her work now became popular, and soon they were calling her the

English Sappho.

Then she had a message from Stuart, asking her to call at his office. With Maria's help, for she was a sad cripple by now, 'Perdita' came back at last to Covent Garden. Stuart asked her to take charge of the poetry department of the *Morning Post* for him, and it was agreed that, under the name of Tabitha Bramble, she would contribute a series of satirical odes for him and also edit the other poetry which he planned to publish each week.

'Perdita' set to work, but within a fortnight she fell desperately ill again, with pneumonia which developed into tuberculosis, and on Christmas Eve 1800 she died.

And it was Peter Pindar – the sardonic old Doctor Walcot – living in his garret in Tavistock Row, who wrote her elegy:

Remembrance shall dwell on her smile ...
Adieu to the Daughter of Love!

8

Change and Decay

With John Kemble managing for Sheridan, something of the old orderliness which had existed in Garrick's time came back to Drury Lane theatre, but by 1791 it was apparent that the building, now 147 years old, was becoming extremely dilapidated and unsafe. It was condemned and Sheridan had to set about raising money for a new building. The second Theatre Royal was pulled down almost entirely, although Wren's foundations were left and still exist. The company moved to the Haymarket theatre while Holland built the third Drury Lane theatre, and it opened in 1794, with a lavish production of *Macbeth*, in which both Sarah Siddons and John Kemble appeared.

The following year there was a disastrous fire at the church, when the roof and painted ceiling and parts of the walls were destroyed. The Lely portrait of Charles I was lost, as well as the memorial statue to Lely himself, with the Grinling Gibbons bust. However, the records were saved and also the pulpit, which had been the work of Gibbons or perhaps one of his pupils. Plans were quickly made for the rebuilding, and again the criticism of its stark simplicity was raised. Many people, including Horace Walpole, had complained that the old church was too severely plain and said that now was the opportunity to build something different, but the architect, Thomas Hardwick, kept to Inigo Jones's original conception and reproduced it faithfully.

Throughout the next few years, no better acting could be found anywhere in the country than at Drury Lane, but all was not well behind the scenes. Sheridan, always short of money, was in debt all round, and at last, in 1805, Mrs Siddons and John Kemble, both owed arrears of salary, could stay no longer. They departed to Covent Garden, and Sheridan lost his two most valuable players.

Kemble became joint manager with Thomas Harris's son, investing all his money in the venture, but three years later came disaster. In the early morning of 20 September 1808, fire broke out in the theatre, and by six o'clock it was 'so completely destroyed that you could not have known a building had stood there'. The blaze was sudden and fierce, and in trying to deal with it, twenty-three firemen were killed by the falling roof. Handel's organ was lost and many of his and Dr Arne's manuscripts, as well as the entire stock of wine of the Beefsteak Club. Mrs Siddons, writing to a friend, said: 'I have lost everything – all my jewels and lace which I have been collecting for thirty years ... all really fine and curious. I had a point veil which had been a toilette of the poor Queen of France, near five yards long ... In short, everything I had in the world of stage ornament is gone, and literally not one vestige is left of all that has cost me so much time and money to collect.'

The sympathy for John Kemble was both sincere and practical. The Prince of Wales gave him £1,000, the Duke of Northumberland £10,000, which Kemble declined as a gift but accepted as a loan, giving him his bond for it. Insurance yielded £50,000, and the remaining £100,000 needed was supplied in subscription shares of £500 each. On the last day of the year, the Prince of Wales laid the foundation stone of Robert Smirke's new theatre, and the Duke of Northumberland returned Kemble's bond, with a letter saying that, it being a day of rejoicing, he concluded there would be a bonfire, and he therefore requested that the enclosed obligation might be thrown in, to heighten the flames.

Several of the houses behind which the old theatre had been built had been destroyed in the fire, so the space was cleared and Smirke's theatre planned with its main entrance in Bow Street. His design was based on Athene's temple on the Acropolis. The four fluted columns of the Doric portico were said to be the largest in Europe, apart from those at St Peter's in Rome. On each side of the portico were bas-reliefs by Flaxman. The auditorium had three tiers of boxes above the circle of private boxes, and the large arch of the proscenium, with its magnificent red velvet curtain, had a span of over forty-two feet. The staff included the stage-manager, pantomime director, property man and call-boy, scene-painters, carpenters, stage-hands, wardrobe-hands, attendants, lamplighters, firemen, porters and box-office staff. The play for the opening night, on 18 September 1809, was *Macbeth*, and the booking was heavy, but when the public discovered that, in order to cover his costs, Kemble had raised the admission prices, there was pandemonium.

As the curtain rose, the voices of the players were drowned, 'in a continuous hissing, groaning, howling, yelling, braying, barking and hooting noise, accompanied by exclamations of "Old prices! No rise! ... No private boxes! ... " The same discordant tumult was repeated on the following evening and innumerable placards calling for old prices were scattered throughout the theatre.' *

For the next five nights the protests continued, with increasing violence, and then, 'with rattles, drums, whistles, and cat calls having completely drowned the voices of the actors, Mr Kemble stepped forward and managed to make himself heard, telling the audience that a committee had undertaken to examine the finances of the theatre, and until they had prepared their report it would be closed. "Name them" was shouted from all sides. The names were declared – Sir Charles Price, the Solicitor-General, the Recorder of London, the Governor of the Bank, and Mr Angerstein. "All shareholders!" bawled a wag from the gallery. In a few days the theatre reopened: the public paid no attention to the report of the referees, and the tumult was renewed for several weeks with ever increased violence. The proprietors now sent in hired bruisers, to *mill* the refractory into subjection. This irritated most of their former friends, and, amongst the rest, the annotator, who accordingly wrote the song of "Heigh-ho, says Kemble," which was sung under Mr Kemble's house-windows in Great Russell Street.'‡

In the end, the public won. The price of the pit was reduced from 4 shillings to 3s. 6d., and some of the private boxes were removed altogether.

After this bad beginning, however, affairs prospered for Kemble. Henry Bishop became his musical director, adapting many of Scott's novels as operas. He also revived Arne's and Handel's works, as well as *The Beggar's Opera*; and under his direction Covent Garden audiences heard for the first time Mozart's *Don Giovanni* and *The Marriage of Figaro*, as well as Rossini's *The Barber of Seville*. And alternating with these musical productions, John Kemble and his younger brother Charles, Mrs Siddons and Macready were playing Shakespeare.

But their old rival Drury Lane was in dire trouble. On the night of 24 February 1809, in the space of three hours, Holland's new theatre

---

* *Illustration of the Public Buildings of London*, Volume 1, Charles Dibdin.

‡ *Romance of London*, J. Timbs, Volume III (Bentley, 1865).

had been totally destroyed by fire. The flames could be seen from the House of Commons, and when Sheridan was told what had happened, he excused himself from the debate, saying that 'whatever might be the extent of the present calamity, he hoped it would not interfere with the public business of the country' and with that departed to see the full extent of the damage. Nothing could be done. The theatre had cost £250,000 but was insured for only £15,000. As Sheridan sat at a coffee-house opposite, with his friend Barry, watching the blazing theatre, he knew that he was ruined. He ordered a bottle of port and, when Barry looked astonished at his calmness, remarked that it was hard if a man could not drink a glass of wine by his own fireside.

Courageously he set about organizing funds for the rebuilding. The money was forthcoming without undue difficulty, for people were sympathetic and generous, but he was never again to be the lessee. The fourth and present theatre, built by Benjamin Wyatt – although the portico and colonnade were added several years later – opened in 1812, during the Napoleonic Wars, with Samuel Arnold as the new lessee.

The Drury Lane ghost, that mysterious figure in his long grey cloak, powdered wig and tricorn hat, who had haunted the old theatre, did not desert its old ground but reappeared in the new one, most often in the dress circle, but with a disconcerting habit of vanishing through the back wall. Several people have seen him, but nobody knows who he is or anything about him, except that he was killed in a duel.

On the death of Charles James Fox, in 1806, Garrick had hoped to become leader of the Whigs, but this was not to be, and this brilliant man, one of our greatest writers of comedy and, in an age of corruption, a courageous and incorrupt politician, died in 1816, at the age of sixty-five.

At Bow Street, Sir John Fielding, with the help of two assistant magistrates, had presided at the court until 1780, and one of his more bizarre cases towards the end of his time there concerned that extraordinary character Charlie Price, the swindler and forger, who made up in ingenuity what he lacked in moral fibre. At one time he was running, with his current mistress, a bogus matrimonial agency in Southampton Street, advertising in the newspaper: 'To gentlemen of character, fortune and honour who wish to engage for life with a lady who possesses the above qualities in a very eminent degree. Her person in point of elegance, gives precedence to none. Her mind and manners are highly cultivated, her temper serene, mild and affable, and her age does not exceed 22. Any gentleman who answers the above address may direct a letter to A. Z., at the Bedford Head, Southampton Street, Strand; and if their morals and situation in life are approved, they will then be waited on by a person who will procure the parties an interview.'

One gullible young man paid 50 guineas for the privilege of an interview with the young paragon's guardian, who was none other than Charlie in heavy disguise, but waited in vain for a glimpse of his bride.

A few years later, Charlie was raising money to open a brewery, which never materialized, and then he ran a bogus lottery office in King Street for a while. He filled in his time making forged bank-notes, but these were his final undoing. He was caught and committed to prison, but hanged himself in his cell before he could be brought to trial.

The year of Sir John's death, 1780, saw the outbreak of the Gordon riots, when the mob, after releasing the prisoners of Newgate and attacking the Old Bailey, burnt down the Fleet and the King's Bench prisons, made an attempt to break into the Bank of England and swarmed into Bow Street, setting fire to the police court and gutting the ground floor. Sir John, already in failing health, was not there at the time, but one of his assistants, who was to become his successor, Sir William Addington, was in charge and sent for the militia.

The house was rebuilt and was to hear many strange cases, as for example, the sad affair of Mr Hill and Miss Johnston.

'A whimsical investigation took place before Mr Graham in Bow Street on Saturday last,' ran the report. 'It was a kind of double charge; the first made on the part of Mr Arthur Hill, of Carburton Street, against a Miss Alice Johnston, a Tichfield Street belle, for pulling off one of his *whiskers*, which happened to be one of the *false* kind, in the coffee room of the Covent Garden theatre. The second, instituted by the lady, viz. that in consequence of this accidental derangement of the whiskers, Mr Arthur Hill caught her in his arms and by a malicious dexterity let her so far slide through her clothes as to make that sort of public exhibition which even shocked the circle of spectators who are pretty well accustomed to *strange sights!* Mr

Hill, who had previously spent the night coolly in the watch-house, being called upon for his defence justified his plea on the ground of *retaliation*; the magistrate holding that the former was rather an accidental assault, and that in the latter there was nothing to stir up His Majesty's liege subjects to any breach of the *peace* – although evidently a shameful breach of decorum, dismissed the parties with a reprimand and an exhortation to better manners.' *

The Bow Street runners, who operated for nearly seventy years, until the formation of Sir Robert Peel's police force, were concerned with the apprehension and detection of crime, rather than its prevention. They were, in fact, a 'special branch', in addition to the mounted and foot patrols which, during the latter part of the eighteenth century, were coming into operation at police offices all over the country.

At no time were there more than twelve Bow Street Runners, and usually there were only eight. Their insignia of office was a small baton, surmounted by a gilt crown, and, like the patrols, they were armed.

In 1828, when the chief clerk of Bow Street was giving his report to a House of Commons committee, he said that of the eight principal Bow Street Runners attached to the office at that time, 'Townsend and Sayer generally attended his Majesty when he was out of town. They are now at Brighton. Salmon and Ruthven have been upon the continent in pursuit of persons who have absconded with property belonging to their employers in the city. They are both returned. Bishop has been at a variety of places in the country – I think three or four places – on business. Taunton has been to the assizes. A little while before that he followed some offenders to Scotland, and brought them from thence. Vickery has been employed a good deal in making inquiries for the post-office, relative to some offences that have been committed there ... Smith has been employed in a variety of matters in Kent and Essex, and at Norwich, and latterly at Baldock in Hertfordshire. In fact, when they are not called out of town to attend to offences committed in the country, they devote their time and attention to the discharge of their duties in London.'

There seem to have been few rules about their duties, and when they were not away on special investigations, they attended race meetings, the theatre bars and any other crowded functions where

---

* Quoted in *The History of the Bow Street Runners* by Gilbert Armitage.

criminals might be found, while one of them was always at Court, guarding the members of the royal family.

The most famous of the runners was Townsend, who was often detailed to guard George III. He seems to have been a shrewd and jovial character, though also a wicked old scrounger. 'This man, who was said to have commenced life as a costermonger, became by effrontery and impudence, enhanced by a certain share of low cunning and low wit, the head of his profession,' wrote Richardson. 'He derived a large income from the Christmas boxes of the nobility and of other parties at whose routs he was employed to detect, or keep away, improper characters, who, he persuaded his patrons, would be present if *he* were not in attendance. As to his personal appearance, he was a very smart little man, clean as paint, to use his own phrase, and I think peculiar in his costume. He was generally encased in a light and loud suit, knee-breeches, and short gaiters, and a white hat of great breadth of brim ... At his death it was reported that he had made accumulations to the amount of £20,000. He was often seen in familiar conversation with George III, whose good-humoured face was convulsed with laughter at his stories.'

Townsend was an extremely active officer, and it was said that 'his name alone became a terror to the wicked and abandoned part of the community'; but amongst fashionable London society 'knowing Townsend' became a cult. Sometimes the note 'Mr Townsend will attend' was even added to the announcement of a rout or ball, as a kind of added attraction. There is no doubt that the fuss and flattery went to his head a little. We are told that 'the artful fellow, to increase his imposture, would, in particular crowds, caution noble ladies to be on their guard, and they would hand over their watches and jewellery on the spot to Mr. Townsend's kind and safe keeping. In the restoration of the articles it was equally the fashion to remunerate Mr. Townsend for his thoughtfulness and trouble.'

He became, not surprisingly, a shocking snob. 'Bless you, sir,' the old man said one day, when he was reminiscing, 'I knew the opera fifty years ago, and then it was worthy of being called a King's Theatre, for only the nobility had boxes; but now you may see a duchess on one side, and a wholesale cheesemonger's wife on the other. I remember the time when there were masquerades, too, and the king – God bless him! – (he was only Prince of Wales then) used to have nice freaks on such occasions. Many a time I have taken him by the skirt of the coat when he was going in, and said to him, I would advise your Royal Highness, if you have got any money on you, to leave it with me for safety; and then he would pull out a purse with fifty or sixty guineas in it, and say, 'Well, but Townsend, you must allow me something to spend, you know', and upon that I used to hand him over about five guineas, keeping the rest and his watch in my own pocket, where few people would have thought of looking for them.'

The pay of the Runners was 25 shillings a week, but when they were called on special duties, the people who had asked for them had to pay their travelling expenses and a guinea a day for their services, while work at Court and at the Pavilion at Brighton earned extra pay. It was customary to give awards to the courts after a conviction for felony, of which the Runners received their share. It was a practice which almost inevitably led to corruption, and the people whose property had been recovered were also expected to reward handsomely.

Townsend, in explaining to the House of Commons committee this system of rewards, said: 'The usual way in distributing the £40 on conviction is that the recorder gives the prosecutor from £5 to £15 and £20, according to the circumstances, and the apprehender the remainder; that comes to, perhaps, only £3 or £4 a piece ... '

Another way of making money was by the distribution of Tyburn tickets, the possession of one of these tickets exempting the holder from having to perform the voluntary guard duties which were expected of every worthy citizen. The highest price for a Tyburn ticket was, according to Townsend, paid by the residents of Covent Garden, where the current value was £25: 'For the constable of the parish must sit up, I think, one night out of three; and whoever is hit upon as a parochial constable says, "This is a hard thing, and therefore I will buy myself off", and a ticket in that parish, therefore, is worth more.' Townsend went on to say that: 'If an officer gets a guinea a day, it is a chance whether he gets any reward; that must depend upon the liberality of those public offices who choose to pay it', and added, tendentiously, 'I am very sorry to say that sometimes they are rather mean upon that subject.'

However, the Bow Street Runners did do some very useful and skilful detective work, in the course of which they frequently ran into great personal danger. Vickery became renowned for his skill in catching French prisoners of war who broke their parole and tried to escape. He also traced two men who, by a trick, had stolen £35,000 worth of jewellery from a shop on Ludgate Hill. He followed them through France and Holland to Frankfurt and managed to recover £20,000 worth of property.

Donaldson specialized in apprehending pickpockets who haunted the saloons of the Covent Garden and Drury Lane theatres. From time to time he used to call out: 'Take care of your pockets!' 'Most persons considered the exclamation as a warning to the unwary,' observed the cynical Mr Richardson. 'Others, less charitably inclined, affirmed that it was a notice given to the pickpockets to be on the look-out and take heed who the gentlemen were, who immediately put their hands in their pockets to ascertain that the contents were safe, and thus furnished the thieves with a clue to where they could get to work with the greatest chance of success.'

Coleman, the last counterfeiter to be executed in this country, was caught by another famous Bow Street officer, Keys. Coleman was tried, convicted and executed, but Rhoda, his lover and accomplice, was acquitted. Keys said that she 'removed the body to her lodgings, and kept it for 12 days. I had information three times that if I went I should find Rhoda coining again, and that the moulds, etc. were concealed in the coffin, under the body of poor Jem Coleman. This, I afterwards ascertained, was the fact.' *

In 1825 a new police court was built in Bow Street on the west side, almost opposite the Fieldings' old house. The new court was described as a commodious room with a bar across its midst. 'Behind the bar, at a table, sits the Magistrate, attired in a Court suit of the days of Goldsmith, and girt with a sword. By his side sits his "clerke", occupied in the "reduction" of the depositions and clad in a gorgeous periwig. The prisoner is guarded by a couple of Bow-Street "Runners", and the general public is represented by some dozen or so of fashionably-attired ladies and gentlemen, who are strolling about and exchanging snuff and pomander boxes, and watching the proceedings with a languid interest.'

Crime in London was still increasing, and with it the corruption of the Bow Street Runners. Only a few years later, in 1830, after an enquiry into the policing of London, the old system of magisterial control was abolished and Sir Robert Peel's new police force established, a far stronger civic force, trained to control mob violence

* Quoted in *Chronicles of Bow-Street Police-Office* by Percy Fitzgerald (Chapman & Hall, 1888)

and deter crime, rather than apprehending the culprits after the event. The Runners and Redbreasts were pensioned off, and the Bobbies took over.

By 1881 this second police court had become run down and indescribably sordid, and the present court was built, on the opposite, east side of Bow Street, near the Fieldings' original house and office. 'Indeed the conditions of the old police court had long become a public scandal,' wrote George Augustus Sala. 'It had changed little, if at all, since Dickens described it in *Oliver Twist*.' This was the occasion when Fagin sent Noah Claypole, disguised as some country fellow from Covent Garden market, in a waggoner's frock, velveteen breeches and leather leggings, with a felt hat well garnished with turnpike tickets, and carrying a carter's whip, to stroll into Bow Street police court and mingle with the crowd of onlookers, in order to learn the fate of the Artful Dodger, who had at last been apprehended. 'He found himself jostled among a crowd of people, chiefly women, who were huddled together in a dirty, frowsy room, at the upper end of which was a raised platform railed off from the rest, with a dock for the prisoners on the left hand against the wall, a box for the witnesses in the middle, and a desk for the magistrates on the right; the awful locality last named, being screened off by a partition which concealed the bench from the common gaze, and left the vulgar to imagine (if they could) the full majesty of justice ...

'The room smelt close and unwholesome; the walls were dirt-discoloured; and the ceiling blackened. There was an old smoky bust over the mantle-shelf, and a dusty clock above the dock – for depravity, or poverty, or an habitual acquaintance with both, had left a taint on all the animate matter, hardly less unpleasant than the thick greasy scum on every inanimate object that frowned upon it.'

'The general air of greasiness and of dirt which hung about it ... seemed to choke and stifle the faculties and perceptions of all who were engaged in its business,' wrote Sala, 'from the Chief Magistrate himself down to the door-keeper. It was, in truth, an evil old place ... '

For a short time, the place was let as a sale-room to a firm of fruit-brokers, and when it was finally pulled down, a newspaper reported its last days: 'The old charge-room is now filled with lumber; the cells, as black as night, where each iron-lined cell door is covered with rust, are not yet demolished. Gaoler White, going over them yesterday, with a reporter, saw some rusty keys hanging to an old gas-bracket. He exclaimed, "Ah! here are the old keys," and told how, in the good old times, when Seven Dials was Seven Dials, and Drury Lane, Drury Lane, he had seen in the passage adjoining these old cells as many as a dozen men, on a Saturday night, waiting for the doctor to stitch up the wounds sustained in one of the many riots which took place in that district, when he was a young constable. "Many a time," said he, "I and others have had to take the boots from men who were kicking the doors, and keeping the other prisoners awake." ' *

All through the early years of the nineteenth century the market was spreading relentlessly, sprawling untidily into the crumbling old houses of the square and the surrounding streets. 'Few places could be more disgraceful to a great city than the incommodious state and mean appearance of Covent Garden Market,' wrote J. Saunders of these times. At last, things got so bad that, in 1827, the Duke of Bedford decided to bring some organization into the market and obtained legal permission to erect the market building. The battered old sheds and booths were cleared away, and William Fowler was commissioned to design the covered market hall, which almost filled the square, covering an area of $1\frac{1}{2}$ acres. The central arcade of double-storey shops was intersected by a similar arcade at right-angles. The entrance, with its arch raised on two granite Tuscan columns and surmounted by a triangular pediment carved with the Bedford coat of arms, matched the church, while the arcade surrounding the outside of the building harmonized with what was left of Inigo Jones's arcades. There were large storage cellars and good sewerage, the water being supplied by an artesian well, so that the market could be easily washed in a few minutes.

The Duke of Bedford, as owner of the land, was given the right to let the shops, to impose market tolls and to make bye-laws for its good government.

A little later, the Borough market was rebuilt, and then, in 1830, Fowler was commissioned to rebuild the old Hungerford market, but although the Borough market was successful, the Hungerford market failed again and within a few years had become the site of the new Charing Cross station.

For the first few years the new Covent Garden market drew many visitors, particularly in the early hours of the morning. Not a few

* Quoted in *Covent Garden* by Reginald Jacons, Simpkin Marshall, 1913

were late-night revellers, attracted by the fact that a few of the market taverns, including the 'Kemble's Head' in Bow Street, the 'White Swan' in New Row, and the 'Essex Serpent' in King Street, had a special licence to open for the market people from 5 a.m. to 9 a.m. How the 'Essex Serpent' got its name is the subject of many fantasies. It has been suggested that it refers to a fabulous monster – a dragon of marvellous bigness – which was discovered at St Osyth, in Essex, just about the time of the death of Henry II, in 1189, although the story was not recorded until it was published in a broadsheet in 1704. A simpler explanation is that it was named after a grass snake which wriggled from a box of fruit from Essex and headed straight for the pub.

The new covered market was reserved for fruit and vegetables, the flower market being held, at first, in the open space in front of the church and round the entrance to the central arcade.

'The effect of the seasons is set at nought,' wrote J. Saunders in 1843. 'In January forced rhubarb is exhibited and French beans at 3s a hundred, hot-house grapes at 25s a lb; in February, cucumbers at 2s 6d to 4s each; and strawberries 1s an ounce; in March, new potatoes at 2s and 2s 6d a lb; in April, peaches and nectarines at 2s each and cherries at 25s a lb, or perhaps 30s; at the end of the month, peas at 9s per dozen; early in May, green gooseberries at 7s or 8s per half-sieve of $3\frac{1}{2}$ gallons; and all the greatest results of artificial horticulture in every month of the year. In January, bouquets of geraniums, chrysanthemums, euphorbia, and other flowers may be had at 2s 6d to 5s each; bunches of violets at 6d each; sprigs of sweet-briar, also the Persian lilac, mignonette, etc. ...

'The carts and waggons with vegetables are drawn up close together on three sides of the market. A waggon-load of fine fresh cabbage, of clean-washed turnips, carrots or cauliflowers, or an area of twenty square yards covered with the latter beautiful vegetables, or either of the others piled in neat stacks, is a pleasing sight. Here are onions from the Bedfordshire sands or Deptford, cabbages from Battersea, asparagus from Mortlake and Deptford, celery from Chelsea, peas from Charlton, these spots being famous for the production of these particular articles, though the supply may be larger from other places. By and by the greengrocers come jogging in; and the five spacious streets leading to the market in time become crowded with a double row of vehicles. The costermongers and vendors of water-cresses, and itinerant dealers who have taken up the trade as a temporary resource, arrive with their donkey-carts, trucks or baskets. The Irish basket women, who ply as porteresses, and will carry your purchase to any part of the town, jabber in Erse, and a subdued clamouring sound tells you that the business of the day has really begun. As fast as the retail dealer makes his bargains a porter carries the articles to his market-cart, pushing through the crowd with the load on his head as well as he can.'

The old market women were extraordinarily skilful in making bouquets for the stars of the Opera House and Drury Lane. The pea-shuckers, shelling peas for the big hotel orders, worked with incredible speed; the other free show of the market was the display of agility by the porters, who could balance nine or ten baskets, piled one on top of the other, on their heads, with apparently effortless ease, and run at the same time.

In Dickens' time there was a coffee-house in the south-west corner of the market called the 'Carpenter's Arms', Carpenter having been a market porter who achieved renown by his ability to carry on his head fifteen half-bushel baskets of cherries from the Adelphi Arches to the market, and throw off one to any number of baskets and never miss. Later the coffee-house became Way's, which Dickens mentions in *The Uncommercial Traveller*: 'There was an early coffee to be got about Covent Garden Market, and that was more company – warm company, too, which was better. Toast of a very substantial quality was likewise procurable; though the touzled-headed man who made it, in an inner chamber within the coffee-room, hadn't got his coat on yet, and was so heavy with sleep that in every interval of toast and coffee he went off anew behind the partition into complicated cross-roads of choke and snore, and lost his way directly.'

'Covent Garden Market,' wrote Dickens, 'when it was market morning, was wonderful company. The great wagons of cabbages, with growers, men and boys lying asleep under them and with sharp dogs from market garden neighbourhoods looking after the whole, was as good as a party. But one of the worst night-sights I know of in London is to be found in the children who prowl about this place; who sleep in the baskets, fight for the offal, dart at any objects they think they can lay their thieving hands on, dive under the carts and barrows, dodge the constables, and are perpetually making a blunt pattering on the pavement of the Piazza with the rain of their naked feet.'

Many of the worst of the taverns had been cleared away when the market building went up, yet a number of streets and alleys surrounding it and the beautiful theatres continued to sink into desolation and decay.

With the new Drury Lane theatre had come a new actor, perhaps the finest of them all, the turbulent, brilliant Edmund Kean. He arrived in 1814, a young man of twenty-seven, shabby, poverty-stricken and already embittered, for his wife and child were half-starving and his elder boy had died, because they had been too poor to give him the care he needed. The other players by no means welcomed the forlorn-looking newcomer, who had somehow managed to be given the important part of Shylock for his first appearance, but when he put on a black wig and beard, they eyed him askance. Even Macklin had respected tradition sufficiently to wear the customary red wig.

Standing aloof from them all, Kean waited in the wings. His cue came and he made his entrance. From the first moment, the power of his acting held not only his audience but the rest of the cast. His conquest of Drury Lane stage was unquestioned, and everyone knew that here was an actor greater even than Kemble, still reigning at the Covent Garden theatre. From that first night, Kean was the leader of his profession. 'By God, he is a soul!' exclaimed Lord Byron, after seeing his *Othello*.

But Kean's early, tragic struggles had weakened him. He could not take success. He drank heavily and became arrogant and truculent. Despite increasing success on the stage, he wasted his vitality and his incomparable talents in the lowest taverns around Covent Garden – drinking and brawling and more than once ending up in Bow Street for the night. Before many years had passed, there came the time when he was too drunk to appear. Although he missed that performance, he was forgiven, for he was still a superb actor, and paid little notice to the younger generation of actors growing up round him, learning their profession and eager for their own brief triumphs.

Drury Lane was badly in debt again. The committee who had been acting as lessees with Arnold resigned in 1819. The new lessee was Robert Elliston, who put on some lavishly staged Shakespeare productions for Kean, but shortly afterwards Kean departed for America. Few people were writing seriously for the stage in these years, for the taste in entertainment had turned to musicals, spectaculars and melodramas. Nevertheless, when Kean came back to

England, Elliston billed him for a new Shakespeare season. Not only was Kean drinking more heavily than ever, but he had become involved in an affaire with Charlotte Cox, the wife of a City alderman, who brought an action against him. Kean became the centre of a titillating scandal. He lost the case, and Charlotte left him for another lover. He attempted a come-back and overcame the initial hostility of the audience, but drink had sapped his powers and ruined his memory and concentration. Before the rising star of a new actor, William Macready, the great Ned Kean, though occasionally summoning his old magic with such determination that it seemed as though he were truly recovering, gradually ran downhill. When his son Charles told him that he, too, was going to be an actor, Ned quarrelled with him bitterly. The sight of the boy's youth and untried strength, his enthusiasm and fresh enchantment with the stage, must have brought him the sharpest anguish of regret for his own destroyed talents, but in the end they were reconciled. Charles made his first appearance at Drury Lane in 1827. Four years later, his father, still struggling to recover his former powers, made his last appearance. While playing Othello, he suddenly collapsed, and Charles, playing Iago, had to carry him from the stage. He died shortly afterwards, at the age of forty-six.

Poor little Grimaldi was dead too. He had long been crippled and unable to clown, and all his money was gone. In June 1828 they carried him onto the stage for his benefit, and sitting in a chair, still with the power to make his audience laugh, he gave his last performance.

The Lane had a chequered career for the next few years, presenting a heterogeneous collection of entertainments, musicals, spectaculars, operas and plays of no great merit. For a time Alfred Bunn was in control. Then Macready, by this time the greatest tragedian of the English stage, took over the theatre for a while, opening with *The Merchant of Venice*.

At Covent Garden, during these early years of the nineteenth century, Mrs Siddons retired in 1812, and John Kemble in 1817, leaving Charles, his younger brother, to carry on. Three years later Harris died, leaving his share of the property to his son, with whom Charles Kemble could not agree. The fortunes of the theatre began to flag, but in 1823 Charles presented a production of *King John*, which was to prove important in theatrical history. The question of historical authenticity in costume and sets was still being debated.

John Kemble had made a beginning. Now Charles, with many misgivings, decided to go further. For *King John* he ordered authentic looking mail armour and thirteenth-century helmets. The audience was delighted, and the way was paved for Charles Kean who, a little later, was to stage his realistic revivals which aimed at absolute accuracy in every detail of costumes and sets.

In 1825 a dramatic critic was writing of Covent Garden: 'We are pleased to observe that this house is gradually adopting the French manner of arranging the stage, making a room appear like one by disposing about it articles of furniture. The bedroom scene had an excellent effect last night, though we have much to accomplish before we can hope to rival our neighbours in this respect. We suspect that the improvement may be attributed to Mr Charles Kemble's visit to Paris.'

Harris's son resigned his part-managership about this time, and Charles continued as sole lessee for a while. Bishop's opera *The Maid of Milan*, in which that undying song 'Home, sweet Home' was heard for the first time, was a great success, and then came a production of Weber's *Der Freischütz*. Bishop resigned, after Kemble had refused to increase his salary, and Kemble appointed Weber as his successor, commissioning him to write *Oberon*, in which the distinguished Madame Vestris appeared. The opening night of *Oberon*, 12 April 1826, was one of the Garden's great occasions and a triumph for Weber, but he was a sick man, and less than a month later he was dead.

Tom Cooke succeeded Weber as musical director, but Kemble now began to run into financial trouble. Gas lighting had been installed in the theatre a few years earlier, but in the 1828-9 season there was a serious explosion in the basement. Kemble had to close the theatre for two weeks, while the old, evil-smelling gas installations were removed and new wax and oil lighting put back for a time. Kemble struggled on throughout the next year or two, during which the Duke of Bedford was putting up the market buildings, but rates and taxes on the theatre were in arrears and then, one day, the bailiffs arrived.

A public appeal saved the theatre. Fanny Kemble, Charles's daughter, revived its fortunes for a while, with her brilliant acting, particularly as Juliet, but it was not long before Charles Kemble retired. In 1833 Alfred Bunn, already managing Drury Lane, decided to take over Covent Garden as well, but his resources soon came to an end, and during the next few years Osbaldistone, Macready and

Charles Matthew, husband of Madame Vestris, all tried their hand at the management of Covent Garden theatre. By 1843 it looked like a final defeat, for no one could make it pay and the building was let for a time to the Anti-Corn Law League. Then came good news. At the Italian Opera House in the Haymarket, which, with the accession of Queen Victoria, had come to be known as 'Her Majesty's', there had been quarrels, difficulties and resignations. The rebels felt that there was room in London for another Italian Opera House, and Persiani, for whose wife Donizetti had written *Lucia di Lammermoor*, found the means of raising money to buy the lease of the Covent Garden theatre and make the necessary alterations, to convert it into a full-scale opera-house.

By 1847 all was ready. The theatre re-opened as the Royal Italian Opera House, the first manager being Frederick Beale. Jenny Lind was filling the opera-house in the Haymarket, but Grisi, at Covent Garden, was proving herself equally popular. Nevertheless, those early months were a struggle, and by the end of 1848, although receipts were £44,000, expenses had mounted to over £78,000. The management passed to Frederick Gye, and at the end of 1855 he let the theatre to John Anderson, the 'Wizard of the North', for a ten-week season of spectaculars and melodramas. The lease ended on 4 March with a masked ball, for which Gye gave his consent only after much persuasion, for it was obvious that this was not going to be any elegant *bal masqué*. The ball went on until five o'clock in the morning, by which time most of the dancers had had too much to drink, but at last, with only two hundred of the large crowd left, the opening bars of the National Anthem began. Suddenly there was a cry of 'Fire!' Within a few hours nothing remained of the beautiful new opera-house except the façade and Flaxman's statues and bas-reliefs. Everyone had managed to escape, but no one ever knew what had caused the fire, and the fire-engines which raced to Covent Garden from all over London, as the flames lit up the winter sky, could do little, for the roof collapsed.

Gye alone had lost £30,000, and with the next season's programme and engagements almost settled, it was a bleak outlook. But Gye managed to lease the Lyceum theatre. This was on the western side of Wellington Street, the ground, on part of the site of the old Exeter House, having been brought in 1765, before the Royal Academy was established, for the building of an exhibition room. It was turned into a theatre for a time and then became an exhibition room again. Madame Tussaud exhibited her waxworks here, when she first arrived in England in 1802. Then the place was rebuilt, but destroyed by fire in 1830. Again it was rebuilt and opened with English opera in 1834, but failed the following year and had to close.

Gye opened his season here on 15 April 1856 to a crowded and distinguished audience, and set about leasing from the Duke of Bedford, for ninety years, at £850 a year, a piece of ground of more than an acre, for his new theatre in Bow Street, which included not only the site of the old theatre but the Piazza Hotel, which had once been the Great Piazza Coffee House, and before that Macklin's coffee-house, and which was now demolished, together with several old houses adjoining it, including Kneller's house, where later Thornhill had come to live and hold his drawing classes, as well as what was left of the north-eastern piazza.

Then he raised money for the building of the theatre, by a series of loans, and engaged Edward Barry for his architect. Although the frontage, with its portico and five great Corinthian columns remained in Bow Street, the theatre, much the same size as La Scala in Milan, was now laid out from east to west, instead of from north to south, as formerly. The Flaxman reliefs were replaced on each side of the portico and remain there still. The panel on the left depicts Hecate in her chariot, with Macbeth and Lady Macbeth, and in the niche below stands the figure of Comedy. Below the portico is the panel showing Shakespeare, with Prospero and Caliban, Milton with Samson Agonistes, the Muses, Bacchus, Athene, Aristophanes, Aeschylus and Menander; and on the right, above the statue of Tragedy, is the bas-relief of Pegasus, attended by nymphs.

The new theatre, which cost £70,000, was opened on 15 May 1858. The portico was originally a carriage-way, under which the elegant Victorians were able to step from their carriages under cover. The crimson carpeted grand stairway led to the long, spacious crush bar, all gold and white, with rose-coloured curtains and glittering chandeliers, and a verandah, now enclosed, which opened out over the portico.

There was room for an audience of about 1,900 in the new house, 497 in the stalls, 136 in the stalls circle, with its 36 boxes, 146 in the grand tier, where there were 33 boxes, as well as the royal box and the Duke of Bedford's box, 144 in the balcony stalls of the third tier, which contained 30 boxes, 384 in the amphitheatre, which had 80 boxes on either side, and 600 in the gallery; but since then many of the boxes have been cleared away, making space for over two hundred more seats.

At the same time as his new opera house, Gye planned the Floral Hall as a vast central flower-market, to be built up against the south wall of the theatre, with its entrance in Bow Street. It arose, on the ground over which so many famous men had passed, like a giant conservatory, with its domed glass roof supported by cast-iron pillars, its central arcade and side walks. It was made partly from materials left over when the Crystal Palace was moved from Hyde Park to Sydenham, after the 1851 Exhibition, and it was ceremoniously opened in 1860, with a magnificent ball. But after all it was not used as a flower-market. For a time promenade concerts and similar entertainments were held there, and soon afterwards a flower-market was built in the south-eastern corner of the market, with its entrance in Wellington Street. Ultimately, the Floral Hall became the principal market for foreign fruit.

In 1880 the piazza west of James Street was found to be unsafe and had to be rebuilt, so today this Victorian fragment, faithfully copied, is the only reminder of Inigo Jones's original conception of what Covent Garden might have been.

9

More Famous Residents

During these years of change in the theatres and the market, a beginning was made to clean up the surrounding streets, many of which, in a grim contrast, were sinking ever deeper into squalor.

Of Drury Lane, Charles Dickens wrote, in 1833, in his *Sketches by Boz*: 'the filth and miserable appearance of this part of London can hardly be imagined ... Wretched houses with broken windows patched with rags and paper; every room let out to a different family, and in many instances to two or even three – fruit and sweetstuff manufacturers in the cellars, barbers and red-herring vendors in the front parlours, cobblers in the back; a bird fancier in the first floor, three families on the second, starvation in the attics, Irishmen in the passage, a "musician" in the front kitchen, and a charwoman and five hungry children in the back one – filth everywhere – a gutter before the house and a drain behind – clothes drying, and slops emptying from the windows ... men and women, in every variety of scanty and dirty apparel, lounging, scolding, drinking, smoking, squabbling, fighting and swearing ... '

Only nine years earlier, when he was twelve years old, Dickens had been taken away from school and put to work in a blacking factory in Chandos Place, while his father, a Navy pay clerk, was lodged in the Marshalsea Prison for a debt of £40, his wife and the rest of the children moving in with him.

Charles's work, which was to tie up bottles of blacking and label them, all day long, had been offered to him by his aunt's stepson, James Lamert, who at the time was a partner in the running of Warren's Blacking Factory. Charles was paid a shilling a day, with which he had to support himself and pay for his lodging; when he was hungry, he would, like the unhappy little David Copperfield he was later to create, 'take a turn in Covent Garden and stare at the pineapples'.

After three months in the Marshalsea, his father's brother paid his debt, and Mr Dickens was released, but Charles still had to go on working at the blacking factory, until, fortunately for him, Mr Dickens quarrelled with James Lamert. Then Charles was taken away and put to school again for a while, but for the rest of his life he was haunted by the unspeakable misery and humiliation of those months in Chandos Place. And although he had happy memories of Covent Garden in the family's earlier, more prosperous days, and particularly of a visit to Drury Lane theatre to see Grimaldi, whose memoirs, many years later, he was to edit, it was the unhappy memory of this corner of Covent Garden which had made the deeper impression. Bedfordbury, then a little seventeenth-century street leading from Chandos Place into New Row, along which he must have passed so often, he described in *Bleak House*, where Tom-all-Alone used sometimes to retreat: 'It is a black, dilapidated street, avoided by all decent people; where the crazy houses were seized upon when their decay was far advanced, by some bold vagrants who, after establishing their own possessions, took to letting them out in lodgings. Now these tumbling tenements contain, by night, a swarm of misery.'

Yet, in its earliest days, this was the street where Sir Francis Kynaston, the poet and scholar, lived, establishing a literary academy to teach languages and the arts, including architecture and painting, to the young aristocrats of early Stuart times, and it was successful until his death in 1642.

Early in the nineteenth century, the Duke of Bedford's Estate Office made a survey of the lodging houses in the area and reported that there were '46 occupied by a poor class of person ... 18 of these occupied by the very poor ... 1 in Rose Street and 2 in Maiden Lane ... the most impoverished class of all lived in Cross Court, Red Lion Court, Dukes Court, Marquis Court, Eagle Court and Jackson's Alley ...

'Most of these people were porters, shoe-menders, labourers, laundresses and charwomen ... there are few of the absolutely destitute class, though the pinch of poverty must be felt, and thieves and prostitutes will shortly appear unless sharp measures are adopted ... ' *

Yet nothing appears to have been done until after the cholera

---

* Quoted in *I'll Fight You for It*, Brian Anson (Cape, 1981)

epidemic of 1850. Then numbers of the decayed old houses were demolished and tenements built in their place, but there is no record of what happened to the wretched tenants while this was taking place, except that they drifted away eastwards. About the same time, many more blocks of dwellings were built in Covent Garden from the endowment of the American philanthropist George Peabody. Those in Drury Lane were built on the site of the old Cockpit theatre, and in 1880 all the eastern side of the Bedfordbury district was demolished and replaced by Peabody Buildings.

By the early nineteenth century there were nearly two million people living in London, and Covent Garden had established itself as the most important centre for the wholesale marketing of fruit and vegetables throughout the whole country, supplies coming in 'by steam-boats, sailing boats, and boats conducted by a pair of oars, by the railways and by land-carriages, from the metropolitan counties, from every part of England and parts of Scotland, and from the Continent'.*

At Number 43 King Street, after the death in 1772 of James West, the house was turned into a hotel, said to have been the first of its kind in London. The first proprietor was a hairdresser from Southampton Street, who could not make it pay. Then came Frome, who had run the shockingly disreputable 'White Hart' in Long Acre, but his new establishment he ran on strictly decorous lines. After him came Mrs Hudson, who in an unfortunately worded advertisement told the world that she had 'stabling for one hundred noblemen and horses'. Then came Richardson, and after him Joy, by which time the hotel was a highly fashionable resort, known as 'The Star', because of its illustrious visitors, there having been seen, on more than one occasion, no less than nine dukes supping there at the same time.

Then, early in the nineteenth century, W.C. Evans, a comedian from the Covent Garden theatre, took over, and it became the highly successful Evans' Hotel and Supper Rooms. It was a favourite resort of Thackeray's, and it is undoubtedly Evans he is describing in *The Newcomes*, when old Colonel Newcome took his boy there to supper and all went well until the end, when the evening was spoilt by Captain Costigan singing a ribald song. The irate colonel, with moustache bristling, indignantly walked out, his cane uplifted, so

---

* *London*, Charles Knight, Volume V (Knight, 1843)

that 'it seemed to fall on the shoulders of every one of us.'

In 1844 Paddy Green succeeded Evans, and in 1856 he built a music hall out at the back of the hotel, over part of Sir Kenelm Digby's old garden, demolishing the little cottage where the Kemble family had been born. The new hall was an elegant room, seventy feet long, with a beautifully carved and painted ceiling, and a gallery in which were the screened boxes for the ladies.

Evans' music hall seems to have been conducted with great propriety, for an account of a visit there in 1867 records: 'Ladies are not admitted, except on giving their names and addresses, and then only enjoy the privilege of watching the proceedings from behind a screen. The whole of the performances are sustained by the male sex, and an efficient choir of men and boys sing glees, ballads and madrigals and selections from operas, the accompaniments being supplied on the piano and harmonium ... On the occasion of our last visit to "Evans's" we heard standard music, English, German and Italian, performed with admirable spirit, precision and delicacy. The performances commence at eight o'clock; and we recommend Evans's to the notice of steady young men who admire a high class of music, see no harm in a good supper, but avoid theatres and the ordinary run of music-halls ... '

It was at a room at Evans's that, in 1857, the Savage Club was established and held its first meetings, until it moved to the Adelphi. Among the first Savages, who could think of no better or more pretentious name for themselves, were George Augustus Sala, George Grossmith, Tom Robertson and W.S. Gilbert. When the Adelphi was pulled down, the club moved to Carlton House Terrace, and then, after World War II, was back in King Street for a short time, only a few doors from the place where it had been born, before eventually settling into its present home in St James's Street.

Evans's lasted until 1880. Then it was taken over for a short time by the Falstaff Club, and later by the New Club, but in 1891 it became the headquarters of the National Sporting Club, which remained there until 1933, when the historic old house was bought by a market firm of wholesale fruiterers, George Munro. The doorway was removed and the ground floor drastically altered, to make it suitable for use as a sale-room, but now that the firm has moved with the market, the house is used for offices, and the frontage has been admirably restored.

Many of the old London coffee-houses had become hotels by the nineteenth century, and although the Tavistock Hotel came down when the Floral Hall was built and the market extended, the Old Hummums lasted as a hotel until 1865, when it was pulled down to make way for new market buildings. The New Hummums, next door, at the corner of Russell Street, was demolished and rebuilt in 1888, but that, too, has now gone.

Nearly every street in Covent Garden has its memories of famous men. New Row, where Dr Johnson used to dine at the 'Pineapple', was the birthplace of Flaxman, at his father's plaster shop, and it was from here that he sent his first model of a man's head to the Royal Academy.

In Bedford Street lived Thomas Sheridan, the father of Richard, whom Dr Johnson often visited. James Quin lived here and also Edward Kynaston, the actor, who retired here in about 1700, having long given up playing female parts, to live with his son who was a mercer; he died here in 1710. Another resident was Clay, who first introduced the papier mâché tea-trays, making a fortune from the two old Frenchwomen, who were chewing away all day in James Street.

The most famous tavern in the street was 'The Constitution', a favourite haunt of Richard Wilson and his friend Dr Arne, and the tavern survived into the 1870s, its site being Number 32. At Wildman's Coffee House, the followers of John Wilkes used to meet.

King Street has many memories. At the sign of the 'Two Crowns and Cushions', where Mr Arne had his upholsterer's business, his son, the future Dr Arne, was born in 1710, and four years later his sister with the beautiful voice, who married Theophilus Cibber, the son of Colley Cibber. James Quin was born in the street in 1693, and from 1743 to 1745 David Garrick had lodgings at Mr West's, a cabinet-maker. Many years later, in 1834, the Garrick Club was established, holding its first meetings at Number 35 King Street, one of its earliest members being William Thackeray; and the club, with its splendid theatrical portrait gallery, remained here until in 1864 it moved to its present home in Garrick Street.

Thackeray had died the year before, when only fifty-two. He had loved the club and was fascinated with Covent Garden. 'The two great national theatres on one side, a churchyard full of mouldy but undying celebrities on the other: a fringe of houses studded in every part with anecdote and history; an arcade, often more gloomy and deserted than a cathedral aisle; a rich cluster of brown old taverns –

one of them filled with the counterfeit presentments of many actors long since silent who scowl or smile once more from the canvas upon the grandsons of their dead admirers; a something in the air which breathes of old books, old pictures, old painters, and old authors; a place beyond all other places one would choose in which to hear the chimes at midnight; a crystal palace – the representatives of the present – which peeps timidly from a corner upon many things in the past; ... a squat building, with a hundred columns and chapel-looking fronts, which always stand knee-deep in baskets, flowers, and scattered vegetables; a common centre into which Nature showers her choicest gifts, and where the kindly fruits of the earth often nearly choke the narrow thoroughfares; a population that never seems to sleep, and that does all in its power to prevent others sleeping; a place where the very latest suppers and the earliest breakfasts jostle each other on the footways – such is Covent Garden Market, with some of its surrounding features.'

King Street was also a street of booksellers and auctioneers, and at Number 38, after Paterson, the book-auctioneer, had retired, the house was taken over by King, Collins and Chapman, still selling books. John Collins had once been an actor, and here, when the day's work was done, he gave his 'Evening Brush', an entertainment of reminiscences and stories about the people he had met during his acting days. Later, in the same rooms, Charles Dibdin gave his evenings, which he called 'London Amusements'. One of the most popular items was his song 'Poor Jack', for which there was soon a demand for copies, and J.T. Smith, in his *Book For A Rainy Day*, says that, 'Dibdin actually hired a stall, which then stood close to the Piazza in Russell Street, such as was formerly called a By-Stander; and similar to those erected in front of the Royal Exchange for the sale of newspapers, being large enough for Wood, his man, to stand in to deliver out the songs. The crowd and scramble to get them, even wet from the press, was such, that I have seen persons fight for their turn.'

Nicholas Rowe, the author of *Jane Shore*, who was made Poet Laureate in 1714, lived and died in King Street, and nearly a century later Samuel Taylor Coleridge was to take lodgings here, from 1799 to 1802, while he was writing his brilliant political articles for Daniel Stuart, the editor of the *Morning Post* who had offered the editorship of his poetry department to poor 'Perdita'.

Coleridge was twenty-seven when he first came to King Street and,

35 The terrace of the new market building, *c.* 1830

36 The Royal Italian Opera, Covent Garden *c.* 1850

37 The mid-Victorian flower market

38 Vegetable selling: painted by Phoebus Levin in 1864

39 Dame Nellie Melba in
1904

40 Caruso in 1906

41 Turn of the century market traders

42 Edward VII at Drury Lane, October 1909

43 St Paul's Church from
the west

44 The monument to Ellen
Terry, one of many
memorials to theatre
people inside St. Paul's

45 43 King Street in the 193

46 43 King Street today; its eighteenth-century façade restored, it now houses an advertising agency

47 The Floral Hall when used as the foreign fruit market

48 The renovated Floral Hall as it is now, with permanent stalls for arts and crafts traders

49 One of the many buskers who find good pitches in Covent Garden today

like so many of his generation, who had preached a form of socialism during their university days and supported the French Revolution, had soon become disillusioned with its results. Deeply shocked by the murder of Marie Antoinette and Louis XVI, he had turned away, like Daniel Stuart, to the more liberal of the Tory traditions of the pre-revolutionary days.

Coleridge was born at Ottery St Mary, the son of the parish priest, but when he was only nine his father died, and he was sent to school at Christ's Hospital in London. And it was here that he made a lasting friendship with Charles Lamb, $2\frac{1}{2}$ years younger, who in the early days looked up to Coleridge as his 'elder and superior'.

While Coleridge was at school, he developed rheumatic fever and had to spend five or six months in the sick ward, with 'seas of pain waving through each limb'. He made a partial recovery but was dogged by ill-health for the rest of his life.

When he arrived in King Street, he had already published his lyrical ballads with Wordsworth, but he now felt that his creative gifts were flagging. His marriage was unhappy, and persistent ill-health and pain were turning him increasingly to opium.

By 1814 he said that he was 'wrecked in a mist of opium', very poor and very unhappy. He made valiant but hopeless efforts to cure himself of his addiction, and in a pathetic letter to Joseph Cottle wrote: 'Had I but a few hundred pounds, but two hundred, half to send to Mrs Coleridge and half to place myself in a private madhouse, where I could procure nothing but what a physician thought proper ... then there might be hope. Now there is none!'

Soon after this, he was received into the house of Mr Gillman at Highgate, as a patient and boarder, and, under the loving care and guidance of the Gillman family, began to write and lecture again; by a tremendous effort of will, he did manage almost to cure his addiction, with only occasional lapses, and lived on with them contentedly until his death in 1834, after which, in due course, he was acclaimed as the greatest religious, moral and critical philosopher in England since Bacon.

During his stay in King Street, at the turn of the century, he had introduced Wordsworth, Charles Lloyd and Charles Lamb to the *Morning Post*, their contributions giving the paper a literary distinction with which no other newspaper could compare. And Lamb was eventually to live in Russell Street with his sister Mary. After leaving Christ's Hospital, he had obtained a clerkship in the accountant's office of the India House, which he kept for the next thirty years, living at first with his old father, his sister Mary, who was ten years older than himself, and his mother, in Little Queen Street, a turning off Great Queen Street, which disappeared with the formation of Kingsway in the early years of the present century.

They were very poor. Mr Lamb, who had married late in life, was growing old and no longer working. Charles's mother was an invalid, and Mary earned a little with her needlework. It was here that the terrible tragedy of his life occurred. There was a strain of inherited madness in Mary, and one day, during a mild altercation with a little apprentice girl, whom Mrs Lamb was defending, Mary snatched up a knife from the dinner table and stabbed her mother. Charles managed to wrest the knife from her – but it was too late. Mrs Lamb died. After the inquest, Mary would have been consigned to an asylum for life, but Charles undertook to be her guardian. His promise was accepted, and he devoted himself to her for the next thirty-eight years. For the rest of her life, Mary was subject to attacks of madness, but they were usually predictable, and then she would be taken to an asylum for a few weeks, until she recovered.

After the old father died, Mary and Charles moved to the Temple for a few years, but they were sad times for they were very poor. Charles's experiments in writing had brought him neither money nor reputation. He was grateful, therefore, for the opportunity to earn some extra money from the *Morning Post*. Between 1800 and 1803 he was first tried as a society reporter, travelling down to Margate to gather news of the 'fashionable arrivals'. This was obviously a well-nigh impossible assignment, as he was working all day at the India Office. Then Stuart suggested he become a dramatic critic, but he had to give up the idea when he could not fulfil Stuart's wish that he should write his notice on the first night of the performance. Coleridge then had the idea of making prose translations of German verse, which Lamb would turn into rhyme. Lamb was willing but apprehensive. Yet 'if I got, or could but get, fifty pounds a year only, in addition to what I have, I should live in affluence,' he said to Coleridge. The translations were not a success, but now Stuart asked him to write witty paragraphs for the paper, about the daily gossip, the scandal and the dress of the times, the pay to be sixpence a joke and no paragraph more than seven lines. Lamb set to work, taking advantage of the new fashion in women's dress, for after the French Revolution the style had changed as drastically in England as in

France. The bouffants and rumps which had followed the hoops and panniers of the eighteenth century all disappeared. Women discarded their corsets and braved the weather in the most extraordinary way, by wearing thin, transparent muslin gowns over the flimsiest of petticoats, although not many Englishwomen went to the extreme of the French, some of whom wore nothing but flesh-pink tights underneath their clothes and even dampened their dresses to help them fall into the folds of classical drapery. In France it was Napoleon who soon put a stop to this fashion; in England it was the climate.

'Since *rotundity* became *grotesque,*' wrote Lamb, 'our *belles of ton,* by *starvation,* are daily wasting their forms to the *sylph-like* standard.' 'Pink stockings still continue to linger out a *lengthened* existence like the factitious complexion on the cheek of decayed beauty.' 'The open-worked stockings worn by our fashionables are truly *Patent,* without even a *Royal* proclamation.' 'Modesty, taking her final leave of mortals, her last *Blush* was visible in her ascent to the Heavens by the tract of the *glowing* instep.'

None of it was very funny, and Lamb found the work a cheerless drudgery. 'As our main occupation took us from eight o'clock to five o'clock every day in the city; and as our evening hours, at that time of life, had generally to do with anything rather than business, it follows, that the only time we could spare for this manufactory of jokes (our supplementary livelihood that supplied us in every want beyond mere bread and cheese) was exactly that part of the day which ... may be fitly denominated "No Man's Time", that is, no time in which a man ought to be up and awake in.'

Yet half a column of his jokes was published each day in the *Morning Post,* and these, with other articles, brought him in up to £100 a year. But in 1803 he resigned. 'I have given up two guineas a week at the Post, and regained my health and spirits, which were upon the wane,' he told a friend. 'I grew sick and Stuart unsatisfied. I must cut closer, that's all.'

Stuart was indeed dissatisfied. 'As for good Charles Lamb,' he said, 'I never could make anything of his writing. Coleridge often and repeatedly pressed me to settle him on a salary, and often and repeatedly did I try. But it would not do. Of politics he knew nothing – they were out of his line of reading – and his drollery was vapid when given in short paragraphs fit for a newspaper.'

It was not until 1807 that the first success came, when William

Godwin asked him to contribute to his *Juvenile Library*. Charles and Mary wrote for him their *Tales From Shakespeare*, Mary writing the simplified version of the comedies, and Charles the tragedies. They then wrote *Mrs Leicester's School* and *Poetry For Children*; and when Longman's asked Charles to edit a volume of selections of the Elizabethan dramatists, his career was safely launched and people of discernment at last recognized him as a profound and subtle critic of English poetry.

In 1817 Mary and Charles moved to Russell Street, Covent Garden, to rooms in the house where Will Urwin had once had his coffee-house and Dryden had held court. It was here that a publisher asked him to collect his verses and essays, which appeared in two volumes, and then he was asked to join the staff of the *London Magazine*, to which he contributed his *Essays of Elia*.

They were happy in Russell Street. 'Here we are,' wrote Mary to Dorothy Wordsworth, 'living at a Brazier's shop, Number 20, Russell Street, Covent Garden, a place all alive with noise and bustle, Drury Lane Theatre in sight from our front and Covent Garden from our back windows. The hubbub of the carriages returning from the play does not annoy me in the least – strange that it does not, for it is quite tremendous. I quite enjoy looking out of the window and listening to the calling up of the carriages and the squabble of the coachmen and link-boys. It is the oddest scene to look down upon.' And Charles added a postscript to this letter: 'We are in the individual spot I like best in all this great city. The theatres with all their noises. Covent Garden dearer to me than any Garden of Alcinous, where we are morally sure of the earliest peas and 'sparagus. Bow Street where the thieves are examined, within a few yards of us. Mary had not been here four and twenty hours before she saw a thief. She sits at the window working, and casually throwing out her eyes, she saw a concourse of people coming this way, with a constable to conduct the solemnity.'

Here Charles and Mary held their literary parties every Wednesday evening, among the regular visitors being Thomas Talfourd, one of Lamb's greatest admirers, his literary executor and the editor of his memoirs. Another visitor was Thomas de Quincey, who was living in York Street, a short street which at this time connected Catherine Street and Tavistock Street. He was a friend of Wordsworth and Coleridge and, like Charles, although ten years younger, was working for the *London Magazine*. In 1821, at last breaking his silence, he began writing, in his grim little back room in York Street, his *Confessions of an Opium-Eater.*

It was on a brief visit to London, in 1809, during his time at Oxford, on a 'wet, sad Sunday', when he was only nineteen, that de Quincey had bought his first bottle of laudanum, in Oxford Street, to alleviate the agony of rheumatic pains in his head and face. For the first few years he enjoyed the effect of the laudanum and the excitement and stimulation to his system, which, he said, lasted for about eight hours. He wrote that about once in three weeks he would 'commit a debauch in opium: and the time selected was either a Tuesday or a Saturday night, these being the regular nights of performance at the King's Theatre (or Opera House); and there it was in those times that Grassini sang; and her voice (the richest of contraltos) was delightful to me beyond all that I had ever heard ... at that time it was much the most pleasant place of resort in London for the passing an evening. Half a guinea admitted you to the pit, under the troublesome condition, however, of being *en grande tenue.* But to the gallery five shillings admitted you; and that gallery was subject to far less annoyance than the pit of most theatres. The orchestra was distinguished by its sweet and melodious grandeur from all English orchestras; the composition of which, I confess, is not acceptable to my ear, from the predominance of the clangorous instruments, and in some instances from the tyranny of the violin. Thrilling was the pleasure with which almost always I heard this angelic Grassini ... The choruses were divine to hear; and when Grassini appeared in some interlude, as she often did, and poured forth her passionate soul as Andromache at the tomb of Hector, etc. I question whether any Turk, of all that ever entered the paradise of opium-eaters, can have had half the pleasure I had ... For music is an intellectual or a sensual pleasure, according to the temperament of him who hears it.'

By 1813, however, he had become 'a regular and confirmed (no longer an intermittent) opium-eater, taking not less than eight thousand drops daily, sometimes as much as twelve thousand', which sapped his energy and seemed to destroy his creative talents. But after he left London, in 1825, going first to Grasmere and then to Edinburgh, where he settled with his wife and family, he seemed, like Coleridge, to be able to control, if not completely master, the drug addiction, and here he produced his finest work, living on until 1859.

Mary and Charles Lamb left Russell Street in 1823 for a house in

Enfield, and two years later Lamb resigned from the India Office, but Mary's attacks of madness recurred with increasing frequency, and Lamb led a sad and lonely life in Enfield, dying in 1834, a few months after Coleridge, while the unfortunate Mary survived him for nearly thirteen years.

There were many alterations to the western side of the Covent Garden area during these early years of the nineteenth century. The old St Martin's Church had been rebuilt in 1721 by James Gibb, but it no longer looked out onto the royal mews and the King's falcons, which had been removed years earlier, but onto a desolate scene of abject squalor, which had grown up on the deserted patch of ground – a labyrinth of murky alleyways and dingy courtyards and terrible rookeries, with exotic names like the Bermudas, the Carribee Islands and Porridge Island, a place which was notorious for its dubious cookshops; to the north were the rat-infested remains of the king's stables, and on the eastern side the derelict state coach-house of George II's time.

In 1829 all this was cleared away and the planning of Trafalgar Square began. The National Gallery was built on the north side in 1838 and Nelson's monument set up in the middle of the square in 1840. Many of the old courtyards leading from St Martin's Lane were cleared away about this time and Duncannon Street, King William Street and Adelaide Street built in their place, but it was not until 1886 that the southern end of the Lane was widened, to make easier access to the square.

In the middle of the century, St Martin's churchyard was closed, and subsequently the gravestones were removed and the area paved over, so it is under St Martin's Place that the remains of so mixed a collection of human beings as Jack Shepherd the highwayman, Roubilliac the sculptor, who lived in St Peter's Court, off St Martin's Lane, Nell Gwynne and her mother, Farquhar the dramatist, John Hunter the anatomist and Robert Boyle the physicist now lie.

With the building of the Coliseum, more old corners of St Martin's Lane were demolished, but Mays Court and the Hop Garden survive on the east side, and Cecil Court and St Martin's Court on the west. May's Buildings, in Mays Court, were originally put up in 1739, by a builder named May, and it was at a tavern here – the 'Sutherland Arms' – that the Eccentrics Club used to meet, its members including, over the years, Sheridan, Fox, Melbourne and Brougham.

During the early years of the nineteenth century the 'Sutherland Arms' was noted for its excellent food, and the head waiter was rated the best in London.

Of the other three courts there seems to be little history, except that late in the sixteenth century there was a private school in St Martin's Court, which Ben Jonson attended, before going to Westminster.

When Garrick Street was built, in the 1850s, most of Rose Street disappeared, but the 'Lamb and Flag' survives. No one is certain why it has the name, for the 'Lamb and Flag' are the armorial bearings of the Middle Temple, but it has been suggested that the tavern was first established by a man who had been a servant of one of the Templars.

The other claims to fame of Rose Street, where Dryden was assaulted, are that Samuel Butler, the author of *Hudibras*, which Pepys tried to understand, but admitted failure, died here in poverty, in 1680; and the infamous Edmund Curll sold pornography and pirated literature at a shop which, after his quarrel with Pope, who accused him of pirating his 'Literary Correspondence' he named 'The Pope's Head'.

In Henrietta Street, the Society of Arts was formed, in 1754, at Rawthmell's Coffee House, holding their first meetings in Fleet Street. Hannah More stayed in this street for a time, and then, in 1813, Jane Austen arrived for a while, to be with her brother at Number 10, in rooms over the bank of which he was a partner. Two doors away, Frances Maria Kelly, the actress, was living in 1819, playing at the Lyceum, at the time when Charles Lamb was writing his theatrical reviews for the *Examiner*. He fell desperately in love with her and sent her a letter proposing marriage, but sadly, by return, she sent him a refusal, indicating that there was 'someone else', although she lived on until nearly the end of the century unmarried.

Adjoining the old House of Commons, in the early years of the century, before the fire of 1834, was Bellamy's famous coffee- and chop-house, where members used to fill in time during dull debates and were served 'some of the best wines that can be drunk in London and some of the best chops and steaks that were sought to be cooked ... The steaks are so hot and so tender, and so accurately dressed, the old Nankin china is so inviting, and the port, the sherry and the madeira ... so excellently bodied for an Englishman's palate, that really now and then a man would rather dine at Bellamy's, than at home,' confessed one satisfied member.

Bellamy's was immortalized in Pitt's last words, as he lay dying: 'I think I could eat one of Bellamy's chops.'

At Number 23 Henrietta Street, Offley, who had once been employed at Bellamy's, set up a rival steak house, which soon became as popular. Offley's chops were said to be thicker and even more succulent, served with shredded shallots and gravy. There was 'excellent dining upstairs, with wines really worth drinking', and it was also a popular place for supper after the theatre.

'There was singing by amateurs one night a week in the large upstairs room' and 'to prevent the chorus waking the dead in their cerements in the adjoining churchyard, the coffee room window was double.'

Offley's was a favourite resort of Charles Dickens, because, he said, 'he always found there a fine collection of old boys.'

After Offley retired and the chop-house was closed, the house was taken by Macmillan's, before they moved to Bedford Street, and many more publishers were established in this street, Dickens' own publishers, Chapman & Hall, being at Number 11, Gerald Duckworth at Number 3, Williams & Norgate at Number 30, Arthur Pearson at Numbers 16 and 18, and later, Peter Davies at Number 20.

In Maiden Lane, where Andrew Marvell had once lived, where Voltaire stayed, at the sign of the 'White Peruke', and where Turner was born, were the Cider Cellars, first opened in 1730, a place famous for its cider and also for its good company, for amongst its frequenters, in the early nineteenth century, were Louis Napoleon, Isaac and Benjamin Disraeli and Thackeray.

'Healthy country tradesmen and farmers in London for their business, came and recreated themselves with the jolly singing and suppers at the Back Kitchen (the "Cider Cellars"); squads of young apprentices and assistants – the shutters being closed over the scene of their labours – came hither, for fresh air, doubtless. Dashing young medical students, gallant, dashing, what is called loudly dressed and, must it be owned? somewhat dirty, came here, smoking and drinking and vigorously applauding the songs; young University bucks were to be found here, too, with that indescribable simper which is only learned at the knees of Alma Mater; and handsome young guardsmen and florid bucks from the St James's Street clubs;

nay! senators – English and Irish – and even members of the House of Peers,' wrote Thackeray.

In 1858, when the Adelphi Theatre was enlarged, the Cider Cellars, which had retained their good name to the end, were demolished, the building which went up on the site, Number 21A, being used for a time by the Adelphi Club and the Maiden Lane Synagogue.

Opened in the same year as the Cider Cellars, and at one time the haunt of Hogarth, Fielding, Goldsmith, Walpole, Pope and Voltaire, the old 'Bedford Head' was demolished in 1870.

It was at the laboratories of a firm of chemists and druggists on the south side of Maiden Lane that, during the latter part of the seventeenth century, Robert Boyle demonstrated his 'Boyle's Law', and on this site now stands the Roman Catholic Chapel of Corpus Christi, which was built in 1874.

In 1820, a poor Jewish boy was born in London, and as a young man he came to live in Maiden Lane as a dealer in second-hand clothes. Moses was no ordinary, seedy rag-and-bone merchant. He was a Liberal Jew, highly intelligent and a fair dealer with a keen eye for quality. He was hard-working and in a modest way successful, and by the time his sons were old enough to help him in his business, he had already earned a name for giving good value. In 1881 the family moved its business to a shop on the corner of Bedford Street and King Street, and when old Moses died, in 1894, two of his boys, Alfred and George, continued the business in second-hand clothes, changing their name to Moss.

They bought the clothes and uniforms of old soldiers and men of rank, whose estates and effects came to be auctioned at Debenham Storr, the old-established auctioneers across the road, and other nearby auction rooms. They bought Savile Row tailors' misfits, which rich and exacting clients had rejected. Then, one day in 1897, a friend of Alfred's, Charles Pond, who had failed on the Stock Exchange and was down on his luck, found that he could get engagements as an entertainer. The only trouble was that he had pawned his dress suit. Alfred Moss, always generous, offered to lend him one from the business. Charles Pond prospered, and when he was well able to afford a dress suit of his own again, he suggested to Alfred that he would prefer to hire one from him, for half a guinea a night, the charge to include the pressing and cleaning of the suit and its replacement when it became necessary. Alfred agreed, and from this simple beginning the largest hire service in the country developed.

In 1899, Alfred and George rebuilt the old corner shop, and for the first time the words 'Moss Bros' appeared over the door. Moss Bros became part of the friendly, generous Covent Garden community, and its fame was destined to become world-wide.

The firm began a men's ready-to-wear tailoring business of its own. When the 1914 war broke out, they found that they had a sufficient stock of service uniforms stored away to open a military department. They bought up cloth, engaged more staff and within a few weeks were guaranteeing to provide a uniform in thirty-six hours. Moreover, they were prepared to equip an officer with nearly all his needs, from a Sam Browne belt to tropical camping gear.

After the war, the ready-to-wear department continued to flourish, but it was the hire-service department which expanded with such remarkable speed. At first men were diffident about being seen at Moss Bros, but as more and more people availed themselves of the firm's service, providing top hats and morning coats for weddings and for Ascot, and expensive Court dress for the rare occasions on which a man might need it, the prejudices were soon overcome. Moss Bros took over the business of Thomas Palmer, the saddler of Upper St Martin's Lane, opened a saddlery department and were soon stocking all the equipment for riding and hunting as well.

In 1939 they were even better prepared for the sudden demand for uniforms, and during the austere years of clothes rationing that followed, they proved invaluable.

After World War II they opened a women's department in ready-to-wear clothes as well as the hire of wedding dresses, bridesmaids' dresses and evening frocks. An American commentator at the coronation of Queen Elizabeth estimated that at least a thousand of the Abbey congregation had been dressed in King Street and declared that 'without Moss Bros Queen Elizabeth's coronation could scarcely have taken place.'

The business has remained in the family, and today five members, all great-grandchildren of the founder, are working in it. The firm now has 660 employees in 58 branches, scattered throughout the country, with one shop, specializing in riding clothes and saddlery, in Paris.

At Number 35, on the north side of Maiden Lane, Rule's is a notable survival of the late eighteenth century. The restaurant and oyster bar were established in 1798, in a building which is now nearly three hundred years old. Rule's claims to have been longer in the business than any other restaurant in London, and is in the tradition of the long departed Romano's and Gatti's, small, intimate and cosy.

Little is known of Mr Rule or the two sons who succeeded in the business, but from its first years the restaurant became a favourite meeting-place of men of letters and the theatre. Thackeray often dined there, as well as Dickens, Douglas Jerrold and a host of distinguished nineteenth-century journalists. On the first floor is the curtained alcove where Edward VII, when Prince of Wales, used to dine with Lillie Langtry. It was approached by a specially made doorway at the head of the narrow, dark stairway, so that the Prince could enter without passing through the main restaurant. On the second floor is the small, low-ceilinged, panelled banqueting room, with its prints of Hogarth's 'The Rake's Progress', and its own treasured silver and glass, reserved for occasions of ceremony and celebration.

A few years ago, the ground floor of the restaurant was extended into the next building, which was of about the same age, but none of the old atmosphere has been lost, and it is still a popular resort of journalists, writers and stage people.

In Southampton Street, the home of David Garrick and his wife for more than twenty years, and of Congreve, Mrs Oldfield, Dick Estcourt and Sheridan's father-in-law, Thomas Linley, Sir W.S. Gilbert was born in 1836.

Tavistock Street, which during the eighteenth century had been known for its mercers' and milliners' shops, also had a famous tavern, 'The Salutation', where the Prince Regent used to meet Sheridan and Lord Surrey, but it disappeared as the street was gradually absorbed by the market.

Continuing eastwards, Dr Johnson, as we have seen, lodged in Exeter Street when he first came to London, while in Charles Street, which has now disappeared into Wellington Street, Colley Cibber lodged at Number 3, with Barton Booth next door.

Catherine Street did not stay respectable for long. Even by eighteenth-century standards it was considered a bad spot, the resort of thieves and prostitutes and even murderers. The 'Fleece' had been closed by the end of the seventeenth century, but the 'Rose', next door to Drury Lane theatre, the tavern from which Hogarth and Gay found much of their inspiration, remained until 1775. Then, when Robert Adam rebuilt the theatre for Garrick, the wicked old place was pulled down.

At the corner of Broad Street and Bow Street stood the 'Wrekin' tavern, where Douglas Jerrold's Mulberry Club met, to give papers on Shakespeare. Later it was known as the Shakespeare Club and included amongst its members William Godwin, then living in Tavistock Street, who was later to marry Mary Wollstonecraft and become the father-in-law of Shelley, but the 'Wrekin' was demolished in 1871.

Many of the old corners of Covent Garden were swept away with the Strand improvement scheme of 1905 and the formation of Aldwych and Kingsway, which so effectively divided Lincoln's Inn Fields from Great Queen Street; and shortly afterwards the Aldwych theatre, the Waldorf Hotel and the Strand theatre were built, the Strand theatre being first called the Waldorf.

The Olympic theatre, which had opened in 1806, on the site of Drury House, was demolished, while the Lincoln's Inn theatre, which had become first an auction-room and then a china repository for Copeland and Spode, had been pulled down in 1854.

The *Morning Post* offices were rebuilt but were moved to Tudor Street, off Fleet Street in 1927, the paper lasting until 1937, when it was merged with the *Daily Telegraph*.

In York Street, connecting Wellington Street with Drury Lane, was founded in 1744 the firm of book auctioneers Baker, Leigh and Sotheby, which eventually became Sotheby's.

Hart Yard, Helmet Court, Russell Court, Vinegar Yard, Pump Court, Nelson's Court, Guys Court and Faucon Court, all little alleyways running between Catherine Street and Russell Street, have gone now, but Broad Court, Crown Court and Martlett Court, on the north side of Bow Street, between Russell Street and Long Acre survive, and it was at the Crown Tavern in Crown Court that in 1841 *Punch* was first issued, with Mark Lemon its first editor.

In Martlett Court lived the humbly born Drury Lane actress Harriet Mellon, who used to cook delectable little dinners for her lover, Sir Francis Burdett, the banker. His wife had become insane, and after her death, in 1815, by which time he was approaching eighty, he married Harriet, who was then thirty-eight. When he died, he left her his fortune of well over a million pounds, and five years later, when Harriet was fifty, she married the twenty-six-year-old

Duke of St Albans, a marriage which, despite all the inevitable, ill-natured gossip, proved to be as happy as her first one. To Sir Walter Scott, a relation of Sir Francis who had always liked her, she wrote: 'What a strange, eventful life has been mine, from a poor little player child, with just food and clothes to cover me, dependent on a very precarious profession, without talent or a friend in the world ... first the wife of the best, the most perfect being that ever breathed, his love and unbounded confidence in me, his immense fortune so honourably acquired by his own industry, all at my command ... and now the wife of a Duke ... '

In 1847 St Martin's Hall was built in Long Acre, as a concert hall, and it was here, in 1859, that Dickens gave three readings from his *Christmas Carol* in aid of the fund to relieve the family of Douglas Jerrold. A few days later he was writing to Macready: 'The St Martin's Hall audience was a very extraordinary thing. The two thousand odd people were like one, and their enthusiasm was something awful.' It was the beginning of Dickens' readings which were to become so popular over the following years, but after 1860, when the hall was destroyed by fire, he gave his London readings at St James's Hall in Piccadilly, where the Piccadilly Hotel now stands. The St James's Hall was rebuilt and opened again in 1862; and five years later, after considerable alteration, it opened as the Queen's Theatre, but it was never particularly successful, despite the fact that it was here that Henry Irving first met Ellen Terry, and by 1875 it had closed and the building became a warehouse.

The Lyceum theatre was burnt to the ground in 1830 and rebuilt on a site a little to the west of the old theatre, with its main entrance in the newly developed Wellington Street. It opened in 1834, still presenting mainly opera, until Charles Matthews and Madame Vestris took over the management in 1847 for straight plays. Its greatest days were to come a little later, with the arrival of Sir Henry Irving and Ellen Terry, who filled the theatre night after night. After their time, the theatre was rebuilt, and one of its most popular features was the Christmas pantomime, but with the outbreak of World War II the theatre closed and later became a dance hall.

At St Paul's Church, the congregations were dwindling, for with the development of the railways an increasing number of people, particularly those connected with the stage and the professions, were moving into the suburbs and coming up each day to work. At the same time, the rising tide of the market crept steadily into the surrounding streets of the piazza, and more and more of the old houses were taken over as business premises and warehouses for the market.

In 1853 it was decided that something must be done about the crowded graveyard, where so many famous people had been buried. In fact nowhere, probably in the whole of London, apart from Westminster Abbey and St Paul's Cathedral, had so many distinguished people been laid to rest — actors and playwrights, poets and novelists, philosophers and musicians — representing all that was best in English literature, drama, music and painting since the Restoration. Now the burial ground was described as a 'plague spot of human flesh and human remains; the narrow place of sepulchre of two centuries of the inhabitants of this parish'. It was closed, and two years later the tombstones were removed and used to pave the paths of the memorial garden which has taken its place. The passage of feet has worn away most of the inscriptions now, but sometimes, as you walk there, the sunlight gives a glimpse of a long-forgotten name or a fading date, which will make you pause awhile and tread softly.

In these few square yards, and in the church itself, lie the remains of Robert Carr, Earl of Somerset, of Sir Henry Herbert, Master of the Revels to the first three Stuart Kings and the last to hold the office, who had lived in James Street, Samuel Butler, Sir Peter Lely, Dick Estcourt, Edward Kynaston, William Wycherley, Pierre Tempest, Grinling Gibbons, Robert Wilks, Dr Arne, Tom Davies the bookseller, Charles Macklin, John Wolcot, to name but a few, all of whom played their part in the history of Covent Garden.

10

Community Life

Gye's new Opera House opened in 1858 with *Les Huguenots*, in which both Grisi and Mario appeared. That opening season was moderately successful, but Gye suffered not only from the rivalry of the Italian Opera in the Haymarket but also from Drury Lane, where E.T. Smith, saying that Covent Garden was obviously catering now for 'society', staged a season of Italian opera for the people, with popular prices – 4 shillings for the stalls, 2s. 6d. for the dress circle, a shilling for the pit and second circle and sixpence for the gallery.

The search for new talent was keener than ever, and Mapleson at Her Majesty's, who was also backing Smith at Drury Lane, seemed to be finding all the best singers and attaining a higher standard of production. Gye was worried, for Grisi's powers were waning. Then, one day in 1861, when Grisi had finally decided to retire, a young girl of eighteen arrived at Covent Garden and asked Gye for an audition. She was Adelina Patti, and young as she was, he recognized her talents and engaged her. The rivalry between Gye and Mapleson was intensified. Then Mapleson scored a victory with the presentation of Gounod's *Faust*, which Gye had rejected. But in December 1867, when the fortunes of the two theatres seemed about equal again, there was yet another disastrous fire, this time at Her Majesty's. The theatre was burnt to the ground, and Mapleson was ruined.

For a year or two, Gye and Mapleson joined forces, but then Mapleson went to America and Gye was on his own again. For the next six years Gye prospered at Covent Garden, which became high fashion, for attendance at the opera in the elaborate evening dress affected by the Victorians of London society, with jewels and tiaras, satins and brocades draped over horsehair bustles, furs and velvet cloaks and long white gloves, became part of the ritual of the social season. They enjoyed the operas of Mozart, Rossini, Gounod, Weber, Donizetti and Verdi, and in 1875, for the first time, Wagner.

This was also the year that the new Carl Rosa Opera Company gave its first season at the Prince's Theatre.

Gye retired in 1877, and his son took over the management. Edward Mapleson, back in England by this time, had raised a large sum of money to build a new National Opera House near the Embankment, but funds gave out before the theatre was completed. The building was pulled down, and New Scotland Yard built in its place. In the meantime, Her Majesty's had been rebuilt and was offering both Italian and Wagnerian opera.

In London society, Covent Garden Opera House began to decline in popularity. The widowed, ageing Queen Victoria never attended, and other members of the royal family showed little taste for opera. The operatic stars, though they sang superbly, were often lamentably lacking in acting ability, and prima donnas tended to run to fat. The real opera-lovers found the artistic standards of Covent Garden disappointing and preferred the productions of the Carl Rosa company, which was now presenting seasons at Drury Lane. Mapleson gave one or two seasons at Covent Garden, but in 1888 Augustus Harris, who had been running Drury Lane for the previous ten years and had been responsible for the Carl Rosa seasons there, now stepped in as manager of the Opera House as well.

At Drury Lane, Harris offered everything that seemed to have possibilities for entertainment – Shakespeare, light opera, grand opera, drama and even nigger minstrel shows, as well as the Christmas pantomime, for which he engaged music hall artists whose names are still remembered – Vesta Tilley, Kate Vaughan, Dan Leno and Marie Lloyd.

At the Opera House he managed to restore its past glories. He had the house redecorated, and for its opening night the Prince and Princess of Wales attended, together with those members of society who inevitably followed them. Harris opened with Verdi's *Aïda*, Jean de Rezke singing the part of Radames. He was received enthusiastically, and a few nights later his brother Edouard had a similar triumph. During the second week, Harris presented *Lucia di Lammermoor*, and the part of Lucia was played by a young Australian singer of whom London had not heard before. She was Nellie Melba, whose success was soon to become as great as that of the illustrious Patti. Not long afterwards, Harris introduced Tetrazzini.

Augustus Harris restored the prestige of Covent Garden, and once more it took its place as one of the most important opera-houses in the world. There had been much controversy concerning the language in which opera should be sung. Hitherto operas had all been sung in Italian, which was considered the only suitable language for great singers, but now there was a change. Operas were sung in the language of their origin, and then there was a movement for some of them to be sung in English translation. With the singing of operas in a variety of languages, Covent Garden dropped the title of the Royal Italian Opera House and became the Royal Opera House.

But Harris's brilliant career came to a sad end, for in 1896, when he was only forty-four, he died.

The market was still growing. As early as 1890 people were complaining bitterly about the congestion increasing each year in the market and its surrounding streets. 'We are fully cognisant of the fact that Spitalfields and Farringdon absorb some portion of the trade in vegetables; but Covent Garden is *the* market, *par excellence*,' wrote an angry Victorian in the *City Press*, 'and it is a disgrace to the metropolis to be compelled to rely on the capabilities of a place which, spacious as it may be, is fitted at the very utmost to serve as a market for a town of 60,000 inhabitants.'

He might as well have saved himself the time and trouble of writing all that. The market throve, and nothing could check it. It was spilling over into Bow Street, Long Acre, Russell Street, Hart Street, King Street, Tavistock Street and even Inigo Place, inside the very gates of the churchyard. In 1904 there was a further extension, when the Jubilee Hall was built in the south-east corner of the piazza, an Edwardian building which in size and style accorded well with the Floral Hall.

Yet although the market seemed to dominate Covent Garden, its literary and theatrical traditions were just as strongly maintained. There was a concentration of important publishers here, and after the end of the patent law many more theatres had been built, particularly during the last years of the nineteenth century and the early years of the 1900s, including the Duke of York's in 1892, the New Theatre in 1903, which after the death of its owner, Sir Bronson Albery, in 1971, was renamed the Albery, the Aldwych and the Strand in 1905, the Fortune, in Russell Street, in 1924 and the Duchess, in Catherine Street, in 1929.

Theatres come and go, and many have disappeared during the last decade of economic depression, yet all these have survived; but at one time more than half the West End theatres of London were concentrated in Covent Garden.

The residential population was still moving away, however, except for the working people, the majority of whom were living in the rapidly decaying tenement blocks.

Apart from the market workers there were dozens of small businesses in the area, many of them associated with the theatres, costumiers, scene-painters and designers, wig-makers, makers of masks and ballet shoes. There were printers and craftsmen, old established food shops and a plentiful supply of pubs and eating houses. It was, in fact, a cheerful, self-contained and busy little community.

With the death of Augustus Harris, there was serious talk of the Bedfords not renewing the lease of Drury Lane but pulling the theatre down in order to make even further extensions to the market. The theatre was saved, however, by Arthur Collins, who had begun at Drury Lane as a scene-painter and emerged as an actor of distinction. He formed a limited liability company for Drury Lane, with himself as managing director. He obtained an eighty-year lease, to follow the one which might have been the last, and here he continued in the Harris tradition until 1924, with bigger and more realistic spectaculars than ever before and more lavish and even longer pantomimes.

At Covent Garden, Harris's place was taken by a newly formed body, the Grand Opera Syndicate, which proved successful and found money to spare for many improvements to the Opera House, installing new electric lighting in place of gas and modernizing the stage, which still had an apron and two boxes. These were removed and the additional space was given to the orchestra pit. A new flat stage was built, in six sections, of which five were equipped with movable bridges. The roof of the stage was raised and equipped with new lighting and scenery, and the wardrobe was overhauled and replenished.

Between 1897 and 1914, during the grand summer seasons, London heard for the first time *Tosca, Madame Butterfly, Louise, Pelleas and Melisande* and *Parsifal*; and amongst the galaxy of stars who appeared here were Caruso, Martinelli, John McCormack and Maggie Teyte. There were also subsidiary seasons, when the opera-house was let to other managements. During one of these *La Bohème* was introduced, and after 1910, when Thomas Beecham first appeared there to conduct, *Elektra, Salome* and *Der Rosenkavalier*, while at Drury Lane Beecham introduced Chaliapin in the Russian operas *Boris Goduov, Ivan the Terrible and Prince Igor.*

The Opera House was also presenting, during these early years of the century, Diaghilev's Russian ballet, with Leon Bakst's brilliant décor, which made so deep an impression in both Paris and London that it began a fashion for eastern styles in domestic furniture and even in women's dress for a while.

Still the market spread. Describing it in 1913, Reginald Jacobs said that, 'the upper parts of the present market shops were once the places of residence of their respective tenants. There are some alive today and who are connected with the market who were born in these minute chambers. It is not so very many years ago that the last person to reside in the market died in one of the rooms, which necessitated the lowering of the coffin out of the window like a safe, as it could not be brought downstairs on account of the premises having a spiral staircase.' *

Although the market still belonged to the Bedford family, it had been under government regulation since 1813. With the dawn of the twentieth century, there was growing resentment that the Bedfords were owners of so large an estate in the heart of London, parts of which were badly neglected and degenerating into slums. They had begun to sell off small plots, and in 1910 the eleventh Duke decided to get rid of the entire estate. In December 1913 began financial dealings with the millionaire Mallaby Deeley for the freehold nineteen acres, which included the Opera House, the Drury Lane theatre, the Aldwych and the Strand theatres, the Waldorf Hotel, Bow Street police station, the Tavistock, Bedford and Covent Garden Hotels and the premises of the National Sporting Club at 43 King Street.

What now would happen to the market? For the first time, there were rumours that it might at last move.

Six months later, in June 1914, Mallaby Deeley sold out to Sir Joseph Beecham, the father of Thomas, who had already had two

---

* Reginald Jacobs, *Covent Garden* (Simpkin Marshall, 1913)

successful seasons at Drury Lane with Grand Opera. It seemed as though Sir Joseph might be about to establish permanent opera in London. The financial arrangements took a long time to complete, and only a few weeks later the First World War broke out.

International opera and ballet were over for the next four years, and the gracious Opera House fell on hard times, being used for a while as a government store.

Never was anything so deserted
As this dim theatre ...
Never was anything so disenchanted
As this silence!
Gleams of soiled gilding on curved balconies
Empty; immense
Dead crimson curtain, tasselled with its old
And staled pretence.

Laurence Binyon

For the Covent Garden Opera House it was the end of a wonderful era, when nearly every year had brought new and lovely operas and a succession of glorious singers to do them justice.

At Drury Lane, although during the late years of the nineteenth century serious dramatists were writing again, their plays were not shown here. Tom Robertson had begun the cult of the new drama of social realism with his play *Caste*. Pinero was writing, and Ibsen's plays had reached London. Bernard Shaw was achieving success, and, of course, his first act of *Pygmalion* was set in Covent Garden. At the same time, the art of the actor was moving still farther away from the old flourish of over-elaborate gestures and exaggerated reactions, in which some of the older actors were still indulging, to the restrained and even casual style.

Collins clung for the most part to his melodrama and musicals, though Sir Henry Irving did a few Shakespeare seasons at the Lane, and so did Ellen Terry. In 1913 Sir Johnston Forbes-Robertson gave his closing season there, opening and ending with *Hamlet*. For a time, during World War I, Drury Lane became a cinema, showing Griffith's epic films *The Birth of a Nation* and *Intolerance*, although in 1916 Sir Frank Benson was there for the tercentenary celebrations of Shakespeare's death. This was the year that Sir Joseph Beecham, quite suddenly, died.

However, in July 1918 the nineteen acres were finally sold to the Beecham family for £2,000,000, the Bedfords keeping the freehold of the Theatre Royal, Drury Lane and the Bow Street Magistrate's Court, while the Beecham family formed the Covent Garden Properties Company Limited, which owned and managed the market and the rest of the estate.

By 1920 the old Drury Lane playhouse was back to normal, with Godfrey Tearle and Madge Titheredge appearing in *The Garden of Allah*. In 1922 the inside of the theatre had a complete overhaul, and soon afterwards, in 1924, Collins retired and Alfred Butt assumed management, launching a succession of highly successful musicals – *Rose Marie, The Desert Song, Show Boat, The New Moon, The Three Musketeers* and *The Song of the Drum*, while the big event of the Christmas holidays was always the Julian Wylie pantomime. In 1931 George Grossmith presented Richard Tauber in *The Land of Smiles* and then Charles Cochran put on Noel Coward's *Cavalcade*.

Ivor Novello's musicals began their long run of successes in 1933, with *Glamorous Nights*, followed by *Careless Rapture, Crest of the Wave,* and *The Dancing Years*.

By 1919 the Beecham Trust had acquired the leasehold of Covent Garden, and for his opening season Sir Thomas conducted the Grand Opera Syndicate. For the 1920 season he took a sub-lease of the syndicate. Artistically it was a success, but financially a disaster, and Beecham disappeared from Covent Garden for the next twelve years. The British National Opera Company, which he had formed during the war, leased the theatre for the next few years, alternating with the Carl Rosa company. Then Courtauld founded the London Opera Syndicate, which leased Covent Garden for the seasons from 1925 to 1927. Another company, the Grand Opera Syndicate, then took a three-year lease from the lease-holders, which was somewhat less disastrous financially than the previous venture but still did not show a profit.

Beecham, in the meantime, formed his Imperial League of Opera and came forward with the proposal to join forces with the Covent Garden Syndicate, and it was during these discussions that the first suggestion was heard of a subsidy from the government, but the negotiations dragged on until 1933, by which time the lease of the Covent Garden Syndicate had expired.

Now there was talk of pulling down the Opera House, to make more room for the market. There seemed no place in our cultural life for opera and too many reasons to explain its financial failure at Covent Garden. These were the days of the cinema boom, for during these years of the early thirties silent films had been superseded by the first talkies, promoting a craze which was to bring to an end so many theatres and music halls. Moreover, radio programmes were little more than a decade old and still new enough to keep many people at home. Lilian Baylis's opera and Shakespeare seasons at the Old Vic were gaining steadily in popularity and status, and during the twenties the Old Vic Foundation had bought the site of the old Sadler's Wells theatre in Islington, where more opera could be heard at popular prices. There, during the thirties, Ninette de Valois formed her distinguished ballet company, which before long was to gain international acclaim and instil in so many of the rising generation a deep love of the ballet.

The country was in dire financial difficulties, and although the economic depression lifted a little, towards the end of the decade, Britain had still two million unemployed. None but the most blindly optimistic could fail to see that a second war in Europe was imminent. Times were grim and the future full of foreboding, and there was little money to spare for the losses which seemed inevitably to be incurred with the presentation of opera at Covent Garden.

However, the theatre was saved yet again. Nothing came of the suggestion to extend the market, and yet another company was formed – the Royal Opera House Company Limited – which took a new lease of the theatre. Geoffrey Toye was managing director for a time, and Lady Cunard was one of the most active members of the Board, which also included Sir Thomas Beecham as artistic director. Extensive improvements were made to the building, and a new block of offices, dressing-rooms and rehearsal rooms was built at the back of the theatre.

Beecham and Toye disagreed and Toye resigned, but Beecham was at Covent Garden until the last season before the war – the summer of 1939. Nearly all the stars of the twenties and thirties were singing at the Garden under Beecham's direction during these years, and for the 1939 season, which Beecham financed from his own resources, Gigli made a return. There were glorious nights of opera during Beecham's time, yet at the end of it all, when the reckoning came, people were forced to the same melancholy conclusion. Opera did not pay at Covent Garden.

With the outbreak of World War II, all the theatres and cinemas of

London were closed for a time. The Opera House, shortly afterwards, was leased to Mecca Cafés and turned into a dance hall, while Drury Lane re-opened within a few weeks, not to present a show but as the headquarters of ENSA. Mrs Siddons' dressing-room, Garrick's room and the Green Room, where Macklin, in a backstage quarrel had accidentally killed a fellow-player, all became offices organizing entertainment for the Forces at home and abroad, and the Drury Lane ghost must have been sorely perplexed at the change.

The theatre was badly damaged by enemy bombing but escaped destruction, and as soon as the war was over and ENSA disbanded, repairs were put in hand. By December 1947 the Lane was ready for another first night – Noel Coward's *Pacific, 1860* – and once again a happy, expectant audience streamed into the beautiful theatre, through the vestibule with its cenotaph and long record of past patent-holders, into the rotunda, with its statues of Shakespeare, Garrick, Kean and Balfe, and up the great staircase into the grand circle, with the portraits and busts of the men and women who had made its history. In 1947 began the series of delightful musicals by Richard Rodgers and Oscar Hammerstein II – *Oklahoma, Carousel, South Pacific* and *The King And I*. In April 1958 the long-awaited *My Fair Lady*, the musical version of *Pygmalion*, opened its five-year run, and then, in 1964, came *Camelot*.

The theatre which began three hundred years ago and has seen so much history and romance, as well as disaster and tragedy, is still the most successful and popular in London, and every player dreams of one day appearing there.

The Opera House too was saved, for during the war the Council for the Encouragement of Music and the Arts (CEMA) was founded, under the chairmanship of J.M. Keynes, with money granted, in the first place, by the Pilgrim Trust and later supplemented by the Treasury.

Sadler's Wells escaped the bombing, and Ninette de Valois had kept the ballet company going throughout the war years. The Old Vic was bombed and put out of action for a time, but the financial backing of CEMA enabled them to send four or five companies on the road with Shakespeare and other classical plays, and also opera and ballet from the Sadler's Wells companies. The Old Vic's London company was established at the New Theatre in Drury Lane, and its productions of plays and operas were so successful that the Government decided, as peace drew nearer, to continue the grant to

CEMA, which now became known as the Arts Council of Great Britain.

This was the first time, in Britain, that the State had ever given patronage to the Arts. Within a year or two of the end of the war, a National Theatre was established at the newly restored Old Vic; and Covent Garden was again the Royal Opera House, for the performance of opera and ballet, the Sadler's Wells company becoming Covent Garden's permanent Royal Ballet Company, while the Coliseum is now the permanent home of the Sadler's Wells Opera Company, under the title 'English National Opera'.

The task of creating a national opera company was not easy, but, under the chairmanship of Lord Keynes, the Covent Garden Committee evolved the Covent Garden Opera Trust, which now works in close association with the Arts Council, from which it receives its annual subsidy.

The market was now run by a subsidiary of the Covent Garden Properties Company called Covent Garden Market Limited. By this time it was by far the most important of all the United Kingdom fruit and vegetable markets and one of the largest in the world, equalling those of Paris and New York. It had become a wholesale market, selling to secondary wholesalers and also to retailers, many of the firms being brokers, buying from bulk suppliers and selling to smaller firms, but some also buying to sell through their own organizations, while others had their own orchards and market gardens, both in the United Kingdom and abroad, for wholesale and retail selling.

More discussions began about the possibility of moving the market. The owners agreed to sell, and the national government at last decided to take over the entire Covent Garden estate, so that the London County Council could control it.

In 1961 the government established the Covent Garden Market Authority, which took over the running of the market early in 1962, its jurisdiction extending over $6\frac{1}{2}$ acres. The Authority was charged with the task of improving the existing market facilities – and now came the words of doom which so many of the market traders had been dreading – 'or providing better ones'.

By this time the market was handling £70 million worth of fruit and vegetables each year and £10 million worth of flowers and plants. There were two hundred firms selling fruit and vegetables on commission or on their own account, forty growers selling their own produce, and over a hundred firms selling flowers and plants, providing such a large concentration of traders and buyers, and such a wide range of produce, that the market influenced the prices for the whole country.

Two-thirds of the value of the produce handled in the market, representing about half its tonnage, was by this time imported. Into the London docks it came, from all over the world – bananas from Jamaica and apricots from South Africa, cranberries from Holland and figs from Italy, lemons from Israel and peanuts from China, dates from Tunis and pistachio nuts from Turkey. Much of this produce was unloaded into trucks and driven straight to the Floral Hall in Covent Garden, which, after losing its roof once during the last war and again during a fire in 1956, had shed all its former glory and been turned into the Foreign Fruit Market.

About 4,000 people were employed at Covent Garden, including 1,700 manual workers. Nearly 1,200 porters worked in the fruit and vegetable section, and 250 in the flower trade.

Throughout the night and early morning a thousand vans brought the produce to Covent Garden, the goods arriving from the producing areas throughout the country, from the Port of London docks or from the London terminals to which it had been transported by rail from other ports – Dover, Harwich or Southampton. Then the buyers arrived and nearly all the produce they bought was taken by road to its destination, so that on a busy day three thousand lorries were making their way out of the market into London's congested traffic between the City and the West End. The site of the market had become maddeningly inconvenient, and there was much to be said for changing it, yet the market people hated the idea of leaving. Many of the porters belonged to families who had worked and lived in the market for generations. George Monro, the fruit merchants, had been there for more than a century. And for all its unwieldliness everyone loved the place, because of its romantic traditions and fascinating history, the jealously guarded tradition of the high quality of its produce, the integrity of the traders and the unfailing cheerfulness of the porters.

Yet after nearly a hundred years of debate, of bitter complaints and stalwart defence, it soon became apparent that this time the change was to come. Early in the 1960s an eighty-acre site was chosen at Nine Elms, close to Vauxhall, which the Covent Garden Market Authority promised would have more space, more adequate marketing, trading and warehouse accommodation, garages and servicing facilities, as well as parking space for 1,500 cars and 2,300 lorries. In 1966 the Market Authority, with the approval of the government, began their plans for the new market, which they hoped would be ready by 1971.

11

New Life in the Garden

What was now to become of the ancient site of Covent Garden? Three hundred and fifty years ago the piazza and its surrounding streets had been planned as the western extremity of the City of London, for the homes of its wealthiest and most distinguished citizens, many of whom had helped to shape the country's history. 'London the ring, Covent Garden the jewel of that ring', the fourth Earl of Bedford had once said.

But the wealthy had soon moved away westwards, and in their place came the Bohemians – the writers and artists, playwrights and actors, the publishers and booksellers, making Covent Garden the very heart of the country's creative and cultural life, and with them came the craftsmen to serve them and live amidst the spreading market and its people.

Covent Garden was now in the centre of the capital, and the land, on which were seventeen theatres and twenty-seven publishing houses, and the headquarters of two national newspapers, *The People* and *The Sun*, as well as the vast market, was worth £2,000,000 an acre.

The 1960s were years of massive development in London. The grim, grey Barbican was rising, to take the place of the desolation and destruction of the German bombing of World War II. Centre Point was built, albeit standing empty for years. High-rise flats were the answer to the housing shortage. There were plans for the redevelopment of Piccadilly Circus, Bloomsbury and Soho.

The London County Council had been succeeded by the Greater London Council, which was now allowed to make its plans for the rebuilding not only of what hitherto had been regarded as the Covent Garden area but of a much larger one – a ninety-six acre site bounded by the Strand, Kingsway, High Holborn, Shaftesbury Avenue and the Charing Cross Road. By many speculators this area had long been regarded as a suitable place for redevelopment, because of its central position in London and its ageing buildings, and property developers were already buying up freeholds wherever they became available.

The GLC was anxious that the redevelopment should be under their control and not be made piecemeal, and in the first place they invited the Westminster and Camden Councils to join forces with them, the new consortium now appointing a planning team of architects, who were given the general idea of what they wanted.

Their first concern was to relieve the Strand traffic, their idea being to make it a one-way street and build a road to the north, through the southern part of the Covent Garden area, and another through the northern part, the two to be linked by roads to east and west, thus creating a circulatory traffic scheme.

Although a few buildings were to be preserved, this scheme would have involved the demolition of the whole of Maiden Lane, the southern part of Henrietta Street and Chandos Place for the southern road, and Great Queen Street, Earlham Street, Short's Gardens and Macklin Street for the northern route, while the building of a new road to the east of Charing Cross Road and St Martin's Lane, and another west of Kingsway and east of Drury Lane, would have necessitated the elimination of both St Martin's Lane and Drury Lane; in the process, it would have involved the demolition of the Adelphi, the Garrick, the Duchess, the Arts and the Vaudeville theatres.

In the piazza itself, to replace the central market building, they planned a national conference hall and hotels, and the piazza was to be linked by the southern road to Leicester Square and developed as a major shopping district, to compare with Oxford Street, interspersed with offices, banks and restaurants, with flats above, while the northern road was to have still more offices, flats and hotels.

It was estimated that the plan would take fifteen years to complete – and by that time two-thirds of the old Covent Garden would have been completely eliminated. The cost was reckoned at £141 million, of which over £100 million must come from private developers, the rest from the GLC and government grants.

The protests were at first slow in coming, mainly because the people who would have been most affected were not consulted and were not fully aware of what was being planned. By those who were involved in the scheme, it was regarded as excellent for the rehabilitation of a highly valuable site, and the GLC began negotiations with the large property speculators and companies, including the Prudential Assurance, Taylor Woodrow, Bernard Sunley Investment Trust, Haslemere Estates and the Bovis Group.

In November 1968 the plan was put on public exhibition. It was hailed with delight by the property developers and also by most of the Press, who eulogized it as a city for the twenty-first century.

There were a few dissidents, but their complaints were not taken seriously, and the Consortium set to work. In 1970, however, after arguments with Camden and Westminster about who should control the development in their particular areas, the GLC disbanded the Consortium and decided to act alone, explaining that property developers would prefer to deal with one authority rather than three. In its place they set up the Covent Garden Development Committee, with 'provision for its membership to include representatives appointed by Westminster City and Camden Borough Councils'.

Many leases were running out in the 1970s, and rents for the new leases were increased. Demolition notices appeared on many buildings. The occupiers of some of the tenement blocks were given warnings that they must be prepared to leave, and the GLC could not guarantee that they would be rehoused in the same area, except at rents they could not possibly afford, since the land was now so valuable, and valuable land had to be productive.

As the tenants realized that their homes were in jeopardy, as the owners of small businesses and shops found that they could not afford the new rents and had no option but to move away, as the publishers and booksellers saw what lay ahead, as the theatre people realized what they were going to lose and the conservationists what was going to be destroyed, the protests grew louder, fortified by a growing body of opinion that, having no regard for the unique character of Covent Garden or the plight of the small resident community and the ruin of the small businesses, what the GLC was planning was nothing more than a soulless commercial development which would make it indistinguishable from all those that had been going up not only in England but in Europe and America during the post-war years.

In 1971 the Covent Garden Community Association was formed and held its first protest meeting, issuing a public statement that: 'This meeting calls on the GLC to publish in clear terms what it intends to do in Covent Garden: to guarantee that the existing residents will be accommodated in the area at rents and rates comparable with those they now pay: to guarantee to people and organizations working here that they will not be bought or priced out by the GLC or private developers and to give a promise that the GLC will preserve the community.'

The meeting was fully reported in the Press. *The Times* said that, 'Covent Garden, once the bright hope of planned comprehensive development in London, has somehow come apart in the planners' and politicians' hands.' The *Guardian* observed that, 'the GLC's basic mistake has been to assume that participation begins only when the plans are drawn up.' The *Evening News* said, 'the whole plan is just falling to pieces', while the *Observer* came out with a forthright condemnation: 'The GLC's plan should be torn up before any more time and money is wasted on it ... the scheme makes no architectural sense because it makes no human sense ... the controversy has blown up over the horizon at gale force.'

Yet the GLC could still give no guarantee that people dispossessed by higher rents could be rehoused in Covent Garden, and the older inhabitants were still moving away. More businesses were closing down, forced out by higher rents, while others of a different type, such as design firms and advertising agencies, were moving in on short leases; and as the building at Nine Elms proceeded, specialists such as photographers and film-makers were moving into the vacated market warehouses.

Siddons and Stirling Buildings, two council-owned tenement blocks in Drury Lane, were scheduled for demolition, in order to prepare the way for the first part of the southern roadway and an extension to the Waldorf Hotel, and the tenants, with the £30 offered to them by the GLC by way of compensation, moved out to find what homes they could elsewhere.

At last the Secretary of State announced July 1971 as the date for the public enquiry on the matter.

The critics of the plan seemed to outnumber the supporters by this time. Strong in their objections were the preservationists – the Town and Country Planning Association, the Society for the Preservation of Ancient Buildings, the Georgian Group, the Victorian Society and the Civic Trust, all of whom alleged that the scheme would destroy not only buildings of both historical and architectural value but also the existing community. The CGCA protested that more houses and flats were needed, at prices ordinary people could afford to pay. The hotels and the proposed Conference Hall were not needed. The traffic plan was destructive and unnecessary. The plan had been conceived in co-operation with the planners and speculative builders and land agencies, with no consultation or regard for the present occupiers of the area.

The barrister for the GLC replied that the plan was for the ultimate benefit of London. 'What you really have to decide,' he said, 'is how best is the momentum of change to be contained. Is it to be contained best by civilising it through the intervention of the Greater London Council, with its control over land assembly, land ownership and leases, or to be left to the ordinary operation of market forces and the hazards that people have to survive against the wishes of their landlords to secure a higher return on buildings preserved and renewed?'

The enquiry lasted for three months, and then there was a long silence, during which more land was sold to speculators, who seemed untroubled by the uncertainty of the ultimate implementation of the plan; more people were forced to leave, because of rising rents, council flat tenants were evicted, buildings scheduled for preservation were renovated and those destined for demolition were emptied or let on very short leases, some of only two years.

But during this waiting period, there was stiffening resistance from the CGCA, the theatre people and the preservationists, and as the building at Nine Elms was a long way behind schedule, the cheerful confusion of the market still filled the piazza.

At last, on 15 January 1973, after two years of confusion and uncertainty, the Department of the Environment gave its decision, the Secretary of State, Geoffrey Rippon, saying that, 'he considered it of the utmost importance that the future redevelopment of the Covent Garden area, following the removal of the market to Nine Elms, should take place in an orderly and properly planned manner' and that 'in view of the special importance of the Covent Garden area, and its key position as an area of major change in the centre of the capital city, the Secretary of State feels that he should maintain a closer liaison than usual with the Council over the progress of redevelopment within the CDA boundary.'

The report doubted the need for the proposed hotels and shops, advised an increase in housing accommodation and recommended more conservation, with 'the scale of new development more closely related to the present character of the area'. The road plan would have an 'unacceptable damaging effect on the environment', and some 250 buildings of special architectural or historical interest in the area were added to the existing list, which alone made the 1968 plan an impossibility, as well as thwarting such plans as the new property owners may have had.

In the ninety-six-acre site of the GLC's original plan for redevelopment there are now well over three hundred listed buildings on the Statutory List. This means that they may not be demolished without special permission from the local planning authority and notification of the Secretary of State. There are also about a hundred buildings on the Local List, made by local authorities. On this list, although they are regarded as of special interest, permission for alteration or demolition is not required. So 'Listing' is a protection but not a complete safeguard.

On the Statutory List in this ninety-six acres are St Paul's Church and several houses in Bedford Street, the Opera House, the Floral Hall, the Police Station and Magistrate's Court in Bow Street, the Theatre Royal, Drury Lane, the Garrick and Wyndham's theatres in the Charing Cross Road, the Central Market Building, the Scottish National Church in Crown Court, the Corpus Christi Roman Catholic Church in Maiden Lane, as well as Rule's restaurant, the Coliseum, the Albery and the Duke of York's theatres in St Martin's Lane, the Vaudeville and Coutt's bank in the Strand, the Lyceum in Wellington Street and the Ambassadors and St Martin's theatres, as well as numbers of old houses in the surrounding streets, particularly in King Street, Long Acre, Monmouth Street and Neal Street, and many of the old public houses, such as the 'White Swan' in New Row and the 'Lamb and Flag' in Rose Street. On the local list are additional interesting buildings and houses, as, for example, in Bedford Street, Drury Lane, Great Queen Street, St Martin's Lane and Cranbourne Street.

In concluding his report, Geoffrey Rippon urged that there should be more public participation in the planning process. The GLC must think again. The CGCA was not regarded as a legal entity, but a few weeks later the GLC proposed the formation of a group of people who were now living and working in Covent Garden, with whom they could consult, and in April 1974, from 4,374 people registered, including about a thousand residents, the first Forum was elected, comprising thirty representatives – nine residents, nine business-owners, nine members representing the theatres, the crafts, welfare and religious organisations and three property-owners, some of these being already members of the CGCA.

Although many of the old residents had suffered much distress during the previous few years, for the remainder and for the newcomers and the conservationists, it was a victory for community participation, and this is how the development has proceeded since then.

On 11 November of that year, 1974, the Covent Garden fruit and vegetable market at last moved to Nine Elms. I remember walking through the deserted market-place not long afterwards, on a dim, grey winter afternoon. It was empty and desolate, except for a group of five or six youths scuffling and fighting each other, in a half-hearted sort of way. Everywhere was silence. Even the scrapping youths kicked out at each other without a sound. The market hall was empty and lifelessly tidy. The surrounding warehouses were boarded up and already taking on an air of forlorn dereliction.

But now discussion began about what to do with the market buildings – the main market hall, the Floral Hall, the Jubilee Hall and the Flower Market.

In regard to the market hall, it had already been decided that the proposed Conference Hall would cause undue traffic congestion and was no more needed than the suggested hotels. It was now a listed building, which several organizations would have liked to lease, but it was decided that it should be converted into small shops. The GLC began a £4 million restoration, and the transformation is now complete. The hall retains its central aisle, and on either side are flourishing and beautifully appointed little shops, with entrances from both the centre aisle and the exterior arcade. In the north row are a bookshop, a confectioner's, a designer's, a kitchen craft shop, a dairy centre, with a splendid display of cheeses, cakes and confectionery, and a restaurant, brasserie and grill, a fruiterer's and a poultry, game and butcher's shop. In the south row are Culpepper's, the herb shop, the Casa Fina, a shop selling beautiful curtains and pottery and small items of furniture, another bookshop, the Cranks' Health Shop, shoes, jewellery, clothes, children's games and toys, a florist, a wine shop and the intriguing 'Segar and Snuff Parlour'.

At the east end, still under the enormous glass roof, are chairs and tables where customers are served from the restaurant under the northern piazza, and at the western end are a number of open stalls selling crafts of all kinds as well as antiques.

There are steps down to a lower court, converted from the old market storage cellars, with more shops, including several dress shops, and with the large wine bar – the Crusting Pipe – at the eastern end.

In the open spaces of the square to the east of the Fowler building and also to the west, in front of the church, a succession of buskers of all kinds, singers, instrumentalists and contortionists, seem to be performing through all the daylight hours and always collecting a crowd of interested and amused onlookers, while up above the western entrance of the building a Punch and Judy show is staged on festive occasions, such as the May Day celebrations, which is in a direct line of descent from the puppet shows which Pepys so enjoyed and which Powell made famous.

In July 1975 the GLC announced a competition for a new use of the Flower Market. John Day, the manager of the London Transport Collection, which was then housed in a one-time garden pavilion at Syon Park, Brentford, suggested it would be an ideal site for a permanent London Transport Museum. The idea received the winning vote, and in 1978 work began on the renovation and conversion of the ground floor of the Victorian Flower Market for the museum, which was formally opened in 1980.

Here you can see buses of the 1920s and 1930s, trams, trolley buses and the first Green Line coaches, as well as a replica of George Shillibeer's horse-drawn omnibus, which gave Londoners their first public bus service. Shillibeer ran his pair of London omnibuses for the first time on 4 July 1829, from the Yorkshire Stingo in the Marylebone Road to the Bank of England and back. It was the first time such a conveyance had ever been seen in London, although they had been used in Paris for several months previously. They were drawn by three horses abreast and carried twenty-two passengers, all inside, for the idea of outside passengers had not yet been considered. The fare was a shilling for the whole distance and sixpence for half way, and passengers were provided with a newspaper to while away the journey.

In addition to the early horse buses and motor buses, there are examples of the electric tramcars which were in use from 1907 until just after the last war, and an assortment of railway vehicles for the underground railways. There is a working model of an escalator and an Underground lift and a display of signalling equipment for Underground trains.

The museum, which has a lecture room and also a coffee-shop, is financially self-supporting, so there is a charge for admission and also for the admirably produced and beautifully illustrated guide, which includes a useful account of public transport over the last two hundred years.

The basement of the Flower Market is to be used for the Covent Garden theatre museum and arrangements are already in hand, most of the exhibits being housed at the present time in the Victoria and Albert Museum.

The Floral Hall is divided into studios at the present time, leased to photographic studios and the like, but some of this space will eventually be taken over by the proposed extensions to the Opera House.

The 1904 Jubilee Hall had been built as a market warehouse and trading hall, comprising a basement for storage, a ground floor, part of which was an open-fronted covered market, and above it a large vaulted first floor, designed as a trading market.

After the market moved, the GLC had planned to demolish the building and replace it with housing, shops and parking space, but in 1978 the vast first floor was let on a short lease as a Recreational Sports Centre, while the western, open part of the ground floor and some adjacent sheds were used as a market for fruit and vegetables, as well as an amazing variety of goods, including antiques and an interesting lace stall, all reminiscent of the old Caledonian market.

The Recreation Centre was so successful and filled such a useful social purpose that the CGCA began a campaign to save the hall, drawing up a detailed plan of the financial implications to the GLC if they changed the site of their proposed development. The Jubilee Hall was not a listed building, and for some time there were grave doubts whether the Centre would be able to continue its work after the end of its lease in 1983, but now the Department of the Environment has added the Jubilee Hall to the list of buildings of historical and architectural importance. The GLC has agreed that the Centre may continue on the site, and plans for the development of the ground floor and the basement are now under discussion.

The Centre is a limited company, run as a collective, and is non-profit making, providing low-cost, community-based recreational facilities for people who live and work in Central London.

Each week some 2,500 people from Soho, Holborn, Covent Garden and Bloomsbury use the hall. In the annual report for 1982, the chairman said that it was being used regularly, as part of the normal school timetable, by the local primary, secondary and nursery groups, as well as the American Community School, Westminster School, the London School of Economics, St Martin's School of Art, King's College and the British School of Osteopathy, for trampolining, table-tennis, badminton, soccer, netball, rounders, volleyball and basket ball. There are special holiday activities for school children, which include roller-skating. The local youth clubs use the Centre, and it runs junior soccer and badminton leagues in conjunction with youth clubs in the neighbouring areas, as well as camping and trekking holidays. The loners, who belong to no youth club, are also encouraged to visit the hall whenever they feel inclined, and most of them soon warm to the atmosphere, which managed to be friendly and informal but at the same time quietly controlled and orderly.

There are weight-training and self-defence classes for women, organized classes and coaching sessions, all at a moderate cost, and for the unemployed these opportunities are offered at a nominal charge.

This is Covent Garden today. The threates are still here. Most of the publishers who have survived the recession have remained – including the Bodley Head and its associated companies in Bow Street, Chatto & Windus in William IV Street, Victor Gollancz in Henrietta Street, Hamish Hamilton, George Philip & Son and Edward Stanford in Long Acre and *The Lady* in Bedford Street, but Samuel French, the theatre bookshop, after more than 150 years in Covent Garden, 83 of them in Southampton Street, has recently moved away to larger premises in Fitzroy Street.

Congregations at the church are small, as elsewhere throughout the country, and today St Paul's shares the service of its parish priest with Holy Trinity in Kingsway, but Holy Communion is celebrated here every Sunday and at least twice during the week; and it is still the actors' church and the headquarters of the Actors' Church Union and the Religious Drama Society of Great Britain.

Memorial services to stage people are usually held today at St Martin-in-the-Fields, but on the west wall of St Paul's are the memorial plaques of famous actors and actresses who have died within the last few generations, including Sir Charles B. Cochran,

Ivor Novello, Sophie Fedorovitch, Leslie Henson, and Bransby Williams. Ellen Terry's ashes, in a silver casket, rest in the south wall, and nearby is the memorial tablet to Dame May Whitty and her husband, Ben Webster.

Many of the names are hardly known now, by the rising generation, but the quotation from *Coriolanus* on Sir Charles Cochran's plaque speaks for them all: 'I thank you for your voices, thank you. Your most sweet voices.'

Now that their continued existence is more assured, buildings in Covent Garden are being restored and reconditioned. King Street looks particularly elegant, with its London International Stamp Centre, the newly painted Garrick House and restored Number 43. Bedford Street and Maiden Lane look fresh and spruce. The eighteenth-century listed houses in Great Queen Street now make one realize how fashionable the street must once have been and regret the Victorian demolition of the Inigo Jones houses on the south side, when the Freemasons' Hall was enlarged.

The story of Covent Garden has now reached the stage of victory, not merely for the conservationists but for the people of the community, for this is a genuine revival and not an artificial, museum-like preservation. Behind the scenes, however, there have been long and bitter arguments. The CGCA no longer works with the Forum, making its protests and publishing its proposals independently, but the Covent Garden planners of the GLC work closely with the Forum and are now sympathetic to ideas which overthrew their 1968 plan, for there has been a change of heart, not only in London but all over the country, towards the grandiose schemes of the 1950s and 1960s which obliterated existing communities in order to build vast developments which had no regard for their feelings and real needs, with high-rise blocks of flats which the tenants soon came to hate and office blocks which, although profitable when they were fully occupied, were often half empty.

As for the developers who now own the land, the economic recession of the 1970s would have made them call a halt in any case, and some have found that there is profit to be made in reconditioning as well as demolition and reconstruction.

More housing has been built in Covent Garden, and plans are under discussion for the conversion of the Peabody Buildings at the corner of Bedfordbury and Chandos Place, the Peabody Trust at the moment hoping to create thirty-five new family flats, with offices and workshops, so that the commercial development will finance the residential development, but there is still controversy over the fact that more than half the development will be commercial.

There has also been a protest that there are too many fashionable boutiques and not enough ordinary shops for the everyday needs of ordinary people, but now that the Jubilee Hall has been saved, the Jubilee Market Traders are planning to reorganize the market, and according to the *Covent Garden Courier* for May 1983, 'It's floor will be flattened and permanent food facilities installed. In addition a mezzanine floor will be constructed above the market to house six fast food outlets and eating areas. The basement will be converted into light industrial space and an office block is to be incorporated; these schemes will, it is hoped, in part finance the recreation development and the building of some flats.

'Next stage for the scheme, which would take two years to complete, is to win the GLC's wholehearted approval that they are ready to continue with the scheme.'

There is a spirit of youthful, happy optimism abroad in Covent Garden today. Even the chimes have been restored to the clock of St Paul's Church. The Garden has become a tourist attraction, but those who denigrate this aspect must not forget the historical associations which draw people here as strongly as the new shops in the piazza, the bistros, the wine bars and exotic little restaurants. These, together with the older businesses and trades which have survived, the film and photographic studios in the converted warehouses, the galleries and showrooms, the new flats and reconditioned old buildings, the little courtyards and ancient crooked alleys which are still there, give a balance which makes Covent Garden still one of the most interesting corners of London, with a vitality fully worthy of its long, eventful history.

Bibliography

Anson, Brian, *I'll Fight You For It* (Jonathan Cape, 1981)

Armitage, Gilbert, *The History of the Bow Street Runners* (Wishart, 1912)

Bax, Clifford, *Pretty Witty Nell* (Chapman & Hall, 1932)

Bone, J., *The London Perambulator* (Jonathan Cape, 1931)

Borer, Mary Cathcart, *Covent Garden* (Abelard-Schuman, 1967)

Borer, Mary Cathcart, *England's Markets* (Abelard-Schuman, 1968)

Boswell, James, *The Life of Samuel Johnson* (1791; Macmillan, 1906 edition)

Chancellor, E.B., *Annals of Covent Garden* (Hutchinson, 1910)

Christensen, Terry, *Neighbourhood Survival* (Prism Press, 1979)

Cleland, John, *Fanny Hill* (Mayflower edition, 1970)

Dane, Clemence, *London Has a Garden* (Michael Joseph, 1964)

de Quincey, Thomas, *Confessions of an Opium Eater* (1821; Dent, 1856)

Evelyn, John, *Diary (1620-1706)* (Everyman edition, 1906)

Fitzgerald, P., *Chronicles of Bow Street Police Office* (Chapman & Hall, 1888)

Hickey, William, *Memoirs* (Hurst & Blackett, 1919)

Hindle, Wilfrid, *The Morning Post – 1772-1937* (Routledge, 1937)

Jacobs, Reginald, *Covent Garden, It's Romance and History* (Simpkin Marshall, 1913)

Knight, Charles, *London, Volume V* (Charles Knight, 1943)

Parsons, Mrs Clement, *Garrick and His Circle* (Methuen, 1906)

Pepys, Samuel, *Diary – 1659-69* (G. Bell & Sons, 1924)

Pope, W. Macqueen, *Pillars of Drury Lane* (Hutchinson, 1955)

Pope, W. Macqueen, *Theatre Roiyal, Drury Lane* (W.H. Allen, 1945)

Pope-Hennessey, Una, *Charles Dickens* (Chatto & Windus, 1945)

The Purefoy Letters, 1735-53, edited G. Eland, (Sidgwick & Jackson, 1931)

Robinson, Mary, *Memoirs* (edited J.F. Molloy, 1801)

Rosenthal, Harold, *Two Centuries of Opera at Covent Garden* (Putnam, 1958)

Stow, John, *The Survey of London, 1508* (J.M. Dent, 1912 edition)

Timbs, John, *The Romance of London* (Bentley, 1865)

Trevelyan, G.M., *English Social History* (Longmans Green, 1944)

Turner, Clifford, *The Stage As a Career* (Museum Press, 1963)

Walford, Edward, *Old and New London* (Cassell, 1890)

Encyclopaedia of English Literature, (Chambers, 1903)

Index